# Pennine Way

## In the time of Covid

### Stephen Platt

www.leveretpublishing.com

**Pennine Way: In the time of Covid**
First published - July 2020
**Published by**
**Leveret Publishing**
56 Covent Garden, Cambridge, CB1 2HR, UK

M

ISBN 978-1-912460-48-9

© Stephen Platt 2020

All rights reserved. No part of this publication may be reproduced, stored in a retrieval system or transmitted in any form by any means, electronic, mechanical, photocopying, recording or otherwise, except brief extracts for the purpose of review, without the written permission of the publisher.

# Pennine Way
## In the time of Covid

# Pennine Way North

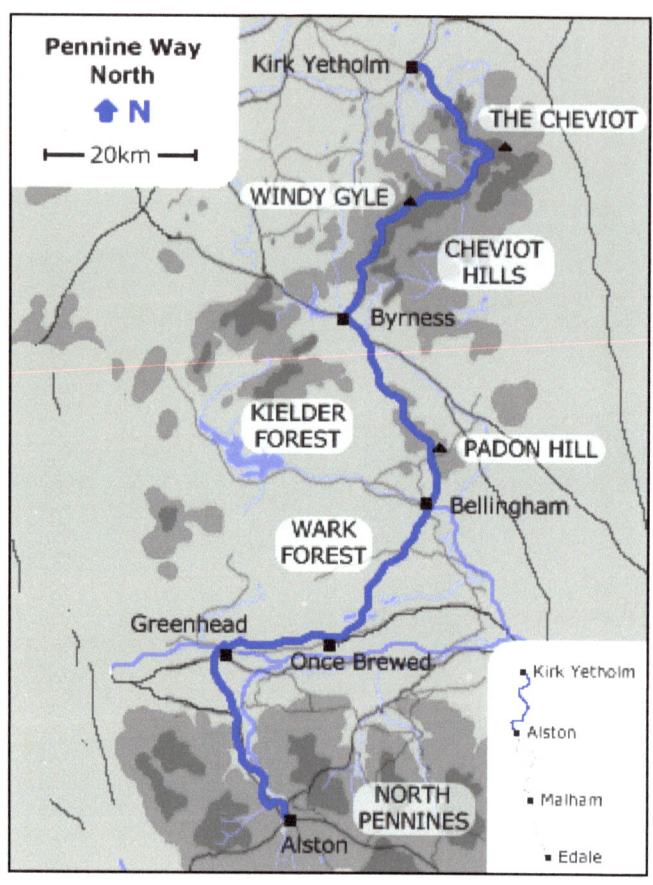

# Day 1: Hethpool to Hen Hole, Cheviot

**Wednesday 20 May 2020    15.1 km, 9.4 miles**

A difficult day as will become apparent. We started well as Scharlie and I got away from Leveret Croft at 8am as planned and had an easy journey up to the border. The plan was to avoid going into Scotland, with the prospect of being stopped by the Scottish police, by going to Elsdon Burn and walking a short stretch of St Cuthbert's Way to join the Pennine Way just a couple of miles beyond the official start at Kirk Yetholm.

There was a narrow farm track that had just been repaired and the tarred chippings clattered on the underside of the wheel arches. We came to a farm gate and turned round and parked in a lay-by. The farmer's wife poked her head over the hedge and asked where we were going. We told her St Cuthbert's Way. She was friendly and explained that the wood the path went through had been felled. A few minutes later she returned with her dog and said we would not be able to go into Kirk Yetholm. She saw my big pack and asked where I was going and where I planned to stay the night. I told the truth, that I planned to wild camp. She got very upset, saying 500 people had died last week. I said I didn't think I posed a risk to anyone. That didn't help. Where have you come from? Derbyshire. And you have to come up here when you have beautiful countryside on your doorstep? If everyone behaved like you where would we be? I'm going to take your car registration and ring the police.

We got back into the car. We'd been eating our lunch of quiche and cheese sandwiches. A hasty look at the map and a quick change of plan and we drove off, heading for the parking place in Hethpool from where I figured I could still get to the Way, even if it was a bit further. We were both nervous and stressed. Scharlie wanted to talk, I didn't. I needed to think and process what I'd seen on the map. From Hethpool it seemed as though you could walk south along College Burn and gain the ridge near the mountain refuge hut below Cheviot. However, this would miss out the first 5 or 6 miles of the route. I'd also seen a small path that went west up Trowup Burn a mile and joined the ridge near the St Cuthbert's Way.

Scharlie read the sign in the car park and pointed out that adders were common and I should keep my eyes open. A pair of swallows that were nesting under the small roof of the sign eyed us from a telephone wire. We hugged and I gave her the guide book so she could follow me on the walk. We set off on our different journeys, me along the private road looking out for the turn through the wood, Scharlie back to the A1. It was a steep forestry track. It was hot and the sun beat down and the occasional patches of shade were a blessing. The dirt road ended at the Trowupburn farm and became a winding grassy track following the course of the burn as far as the ridge. A solitary walker passed heading north – the only person I saw all day.

The Way was a welcome sight and I had half an hour's rest in the heather dozing off to the song of skylarks. The way rose steadily to Black Hag. The peat, that looks as though it could be a quagmire at times, was bone dry. There were occasional stretches of stone slab to convince me I was on the right track, but I was amazed how untrodden the path seemed; an indistinct sheep track at times. The pull up to the Schil (605 m) was hard and I was very slow, stopping more than usual. But I finally made it and climbed the stile and found a sheltered spot beyond the rocky summit to lie down again and snooze. I had a scramble to the summit before retracing my steps to the stile and regaining the path, which eventually led to the mountain bothy. I went in. There was a

*Trowupburn farm, near Hethpool, at the start of the walk*

narrow wooden bench on three sides and a concrete floor. I contemplated spending the night here, but there was no water. So I consulted the map and looked at the terrain and decided to press on the mile or so to Hen Hole, the ravine before Cheviot.

A couple of hundred metres below the path I found a flat soft patch and dropped the sack and changed my boots for Crocs. I fetched out my three water bottles and headed off down the slope till I gained the track down College Burn. I descended a long way and then traversed to the stream and found abundant water and filled my bottles. Contouring back up the hill a short brown snake scooted from under my feet into the grass. Maybe Scharlie had been right to warn me about adders. I set up my solar panel and connected my battery and made dinner – chicken with rice, a pot of tea and an oat bar. I texted Scharlie and fortunately she had just got home safely. The signal is poor and intermittent. I had taken out the tent but had decided against erecting it, thinking I might try sleeping out.

There are grouse gobbling in the ravine as I write. The sun is about to set. It was chilly but very comfortable on the dry cotton grass and peat. A hard but promising day and I'm established on the route. It's a good time to come – the solitude is extraordinary, only the curlew, pipits and grouse for company.

*First night's bivvi sleeping out amongst the soft cotton grass at Hen Hole*

# Day 2: Hen Hole to Byrness

**Thursday 21 May 2020  31.9 km, 19.8 miles**

I woke at 5am. and made a move, putting in my eyes and then making a brew and eating my oat breakfast with nuts and raisins, dried apple, banana and raspberries. I set off slowly up the slope to the cairn at the top of Hen Hole. There was a stonewall shelter and I stopped for a quick rest and to take stock. I came to the sign to Cheviot summit which said 1 1/2 miles; it looked further and I thought I'd give it a miss. This is a most exciting part of the walk and I was, despite tired legs and sore shoulders, enjoying the isolation and the unspoiled character of the trail. Maybe it's more of a motorway further south, but here it's delightfully untrammelled.

There was a cuckoo in the distant wood near King's Seat and a straggling flock of seagulls crossing the ridge, going west near Cannell Street, a drovers' road over a coll. Perhaps a hundred crossed over in small groups. There were more gulls crossing at Windy Gyll. The track was broad and green here and

*Sign to Cheviot, as close as I got to the summit of Cheviot*

I took the less travelled branch on the Scottish side of the fence line. It's interesting – the border is a simple wire fence with gates every so often. This borderland is fascinating. It must have meant a lot to the Romans, looking apprehensively north. It's been a significant landscape for drovers and reivers, for barons and sovereigns. I thought of the men driving cattle south to market, where did they sleep and how, what did they carry and what did they eat? I bet they travelled much lighter than I am.

There was a herd of goats near Mozie Law but they moved off to dead ground as soon as they saw me, following a large ram. There were pheasant feathers near a stile and I imagined a fox or a raptor; most probably a hawk, maybe a hen harrier. The one I'd seen in Ashop Clough on one of my training walks looked big enough to tackle a pheasant. I picked up the two long tail feathers and stuck them into the top of my sack along with my Crocs. At the point where the Way crosses the Street, another drovers' road, I saw an elderly man who'd walked up from the south. We exchanged greetings and I watched him into the distance as I sat, resting, on a stile.

I was getting tired up Beefstand Hill yet pressed on to Lamb Hill along a paved path. Many of the tops have little granite outcrops. That's why they are summits, I thought, because the hard rock stopped erosion. Pity there are no

*Lamb Hill. Stone slabs have been the saving of the Way*

cliffs, since the grey rock looks very climbable. I rested a while in the refuge at the foot of Lamb Hill, making coffee and having lunch – some of the lomo embuchado. I sat outside in the sun and wind writing my journal.

From the refuge there is a long and fairly flat section that must be boggy in wet weather. Today it is mercifully dry. A family of goats on the path spotted me and sped away. The billy with his venerable beard caught them up and led them away into the gorse. I spotted more families on the fence line. I expect they're wild. Scharlie texted to suggest I might take a shortcut and not go to the Roman camp at Chew Green. At the Roman signalling station, a mile above the camp, there is path that goes directly to Croquet Head. But I was short of water so I decided to continue on the normal route. There was good water and a sheltered sward of grass next to the river but no phone signal. Since Scharlie would be worried, I pressed on. It seemed a long way to Croquet Head but the climb up Ogre Hill wasn't as bad as I feared and I made it to Ravens Knowe (Pike) and took off my boots and had an oat bar to give me energy to get to Byrness. A man arrived and asked if there was a loop back so he didn't have to retrace his steps. I looked at the map and suggestion he go east and drop down to a farm track and so back a different way.

It would have been pleasant meandering along the grassy track between the

*St Francis's Church in Byrness, the first village I came to*

tops of Hows Howe and Byrness Hill if I hadn't been so tired. The drop off the ridge was steep and I had to watch my step. A fall here would be a bad idea. Then through the pinewoods to the road. Byrness village is strung out like a Scottish village.

I walked on a path by the stream taking photographs to show Scharlie when I got back — meadow buttercup. stitchwort, meadow sweet, lady's smock, lady's mantle and water avens. Finally I made it to the public toilets I'd seen on the map, which were locked, of course. But there were picnic benches and a flat lawn. I fetched water from the stream, put in two tablets and boiled it vigorously and had my meal of spaghetti Bolognese and a mug of tea. It was getting dark as I put up the tent and wrote up my journal. It rained in the night but I slept well.

*Camp behind the loos in Blakehopeburnhaugh, Byrness*

# Day 3: Byrness to Hazel Burn, Bellingham

**Friday 22 May 2020   18.8 km, 11.7 miles**

I woke at 6 but it was raining, so I dozed till 8 by which time it had stopped raining and the tent had dried. I packed quickly and went to fetch more water as Scharlie had texted to say there wasn't any today. It was sunny but the wind was strong even in the sheltered spot. John texted to say he was following me on Strava. If I have an accident he would know exactly where I was. I'm glad he's made the effort. The wide forest track led steadily upwards for what seemed mile after mile. There was birdsong and the foresters had left a wide margin either side of the path for birch and willow. I was just getting bored of endless forest when I caught sight of something russet and white bounding through the tussock grass. A dog? Here? It stopped on the road and stood stock still. It was a golden fox. A big male, strong, huge, coloured red, tawny and gold. It was magical. It sensed something but the wind was towards me. Gingerly I took up my camera. As soon as I pointed it was off, disappearing

*Tedious stoney track through felled forestry*

in an instant.

The trees thinned – good to be out of the dark green, and the track narrowed but was still stone and difficult to walk on in the strong west wind that pushed me sideways off my feet. A rain shower came and I stopped and put on my anorak and short gaiters to stop my socks getting soaked from the water running down my bare legs. Finally I was out of the forestry land and the track narrowed to a steep path with uneven stones. There was a stone path across a boggy area and an easy climb to Padon Hill. The track is delightfully narrow and untrammeled here.

I was hoping to find a stone wall to hide behind out of the wind and have a break, but it was all wire fences. I saw a small rock, only 3 feet high, but with a soft grassy dip behind it out of the wind. Taking off my pack I lay down with my head on the sack and rested. It was early for lunch but I figured this might be the only shelter I'd find so I got out the lomo and oat bar and ate. As I was wrapping the meat a gust ripped the plastic bag and cling film out of my hands and away. Luckily it caught on a wire fence and I was able to retrieve it.

I came to a road and crossed and climbed easily to Whitley Pike. There was a stone with PW carved on it and a grassy path leading off that I followed. Scharlie texted to say I should bear right at the summit. I'd gone straight on. I

*Whitley Pike where I went wrong following a bright green path*

thought to go back but decided to go down to the Black Sike and see. There was a concrete bridge but no path on the other side. I had gone wrong. Seduced again by the soft green way. Go back or go on? I figured I could ascend in a diagonal line and hit the path. It was difficult walking in the teeth of the gale over the hummocky grass and heather. I must have missed the path. I was lost.

I could see a post on Deer Play, the next top. Go for it over difficult ground or cast back and find the path? I got to the sinkholes, marked on my map and blissfully out of the wind and got out the map for the first time. Impossible earlier. I should be right on the path. There was a faint line so I followed it and eventually found a marker post and a clear wide path. It was then plain sailing to Lough Shaw, past grouse butts to the road.

Across the road, a wide grassy path curves off right. A hail shower passed and I turned away from it and cowered under my hood. I reached Hareshaw House and beyond, on the open moor, came to a bridge over a delightful brook. There was a sheltered spot next to the water and I lay down in the sun out of the wind and talked briefly to Scharlie. She said I'd have to go a long way past Bellingham to find anywhere to camp. I looked on the map and could see no water for a good while.

*Regaining the path after getting lost in mist on Black Sike*

Managing the water and keeping my phone charged are among my daily preoccupations, as are my aches and pains of course. As you walk your mind works, assessing how you're doing, noticing twinges in muscles, pain in hip and arthritic feet, boots rubbing, shoulders aching. Will your body hold up? You play with the idea of giving up. I could stop at the road, pitch the tent and wait for Scharlie to come and get me! Nevertheless, I carried on.

I pitched the tent. It was in distant view of Hareshaw House, but I hoped it would be all right. I decided it was better the other way so I re-pitched it and got out my things. I'm down at the stream. I've made coffee and had an oat bar. I've bathed my feet and I'm feeling good. It's getting chilly so I'll get back in the tent. Tomorrow is another day to Hadrian's Wall.

*Hazel Burn, near Hareshaw House, with good clean water and a sheltered site*

# Day 4: Hazel Burn to Cawfield Quarry, Hadrian's Wall

**Saturday 23 May 2020   18.8 km, 11.7 mile**

I woke at 5.30 to light rain and a rainbow. The sky cleared and I was able to pack in the dry and got away soon after 6. I had just left when a ginger spaniel arrived followed by a black mongrel then a man in long boots.

   You must have walked all night, he said.

   I stopped by the stream, it was the only sheltered spot with water.

   I'll catch you up on the way back, he said in a friendly way. He did and it was useful following in his footsteps across the bog. I could see Bellingham, quite a large village below me.

   He was waiting from me as I got into the village and gave me directions. Turn left at the T-junction and cross the Tyne Bridge. Don't take all the back alleys, as you will get lost. I like this Northumbrian accent, like a soft Geordie. Passing the Heritage Centre I noticed a bench and another tucked in out of the wind, which was growing stronger now. I made breakfast, brewed up and

*Dawn at Hazel Burn camp*

*Heritage Centre, Bellingham, where I managed to make breakfast out of the wind*

*Deserted Bellingham centre early in the morning*

had a rest reading the notices about the history of Bellingham pinned on the inside of the windows of the centre – all shut up with Covid.

The directions may have been my undoing because I didn't look at the map – map reading is almost impossible in a strong wind – and I turned right instead of left. I realised after half a mile and turned back and went through the village. By now the general store was open and the proprietor smiled at me. I thought to go and buy a lighter to replace the one that had failed. I was having to use matches.

Then I noticed the bread shop was open and went over to look in the window and saw they had pasties. Do you take cards for a pasty. We don't take cards for anything. There's a cash machine next door. I returned with a freshly minted £10 note.

Do you want it hot?

No it will be cold by the time I eat it.

Are you doing the Pennine Way.

Yes I am.

I didn't know the paths were open.

With Covid?

Yes.

*St Cuthbert's and Black Bull Hotel, Manchester Square, Bellingham*

Stay safe, stay alert!

Stay at home is better!

At the Tyne Bridge a magnificent sandstone arch structure, I took off my pack and dropped down to the river to the alternative path to take a photograph. At the cemetery chapel I noticed that the door was open. It was blowing hard and raining so I went in and took off my sack and sat in a pew and contemplated the stained glass gable end window.

It's about a mile along the road until the path dives off into the fields and climbs to the road leading to the radio mast. The path winds down Shitlington Crag and passes a delightful house that has chairs and benches for walkers. I stopped and rested a moment. I met a man walking his dog and he told me, when you hit the metal road go straight on.

In the open fields there were cattle with calves and a prize golden bull. Then two beautiful chestnut horses gamboling in a hillside field. This is rich farming country. The navigation was complex from farm to farm. Yet strangely, the only time I got lost, was in the village! Then there were stretches of forest. It's not so nice walking forest trails; they are either wide stone tracks built for heavy traffic, not walkers, or indistinct forest paths that are boggy and bumpy with tree roots. But I welcomed the respite from the gale. I stopped as soon as I

*Tyne Bridge, Bellingham*

reached the forest edge and found a grassy space between the fence line and the trees and had lunch.

It seemed a long way but finally I reached the pull up to the wall. This was familiar territory. Scharlie and I had walked three days of the central section of the wall with our German friend Axel in May 2017. I thought I might get water here. So I hadn't filled up at the couple of streams I passed. A mistake. This was to be the hardest section to date.

The wind was gale force by now blowing from the West and I had to walk into the teeth of it. It was an effort making each footstep. It was cold and there were biting gusts of rain. The wall goes up and down, quite steeply in places. I passed a grassy dip out of the wind, but couldn't stop as I had no water. So I pressed on, each mile seemingly endless. I thought of running a four-minute mile. Mine felt like a four-hour mile. I passed the famous sycamore tree in a gap in the Wall and sent Scharlie a photograph, and then Craig Lough. In a clump of trees at Steel Rigg thirty or so swallows were doing acrobatics, surfing and swooping close to the ground and weaving between the trees most beautifully. And a murder of crows were being tossed about in the gale above us.

At Windshield's Crag, the highest part of the wall, I could hardly stand. I only

*Chairs put out for walkers at Linacres*

kept going because there was no alternative. I crossed through Caw Gap were the road pierces the wall and three-quarters of a mile further on found water in Cawfield Quarry. My battery was finished and I only had 20% on the phone. Strava really eats up the battery. If it isn't sunny tomorrow I'm in trouble. I skirted the lake and found a green patch of lawn to pitch the tent. I scrambled down to the lake to fill my water bottles then stumbled and fell climbing back up the steep bank with my hands full. The gale whipped my Crocs and the two pheasant feathers off the back of my pack. I found the Crocs but one of the feathers was lost. Nevermind, I thought. I still have one.

After pitching the tent, I climbed a hill behind the quarry to ring Scharlie since I couldn't get a signal below. She was pleased I was safe and said did I know it was a bank holiday on Monday and I would arrive in Alston too early. Oh dear. Best laid plans. I cooked, wrote up and got to bed.

*Sycamore Gap "Robin Hood Tree", Hadrian's Wall*

# Day 5: Cawfield Quarry to Kellah Burn, Upham

**Sunday 24 May 2020   14.7 km, 9.2 miles**

I couldn't find my eye mask and assumed I'd wake early, but it was 6.30 when I woke and checked my watch. I've had my duvet jacket on in bed and was warm for the first time. Outside it was grey and drizzling. I packed the tent and made a brew and breakfast. I carried my gear over to the loos and folded my tent on a handy picnic table under a porch roof. There was a tap on a wall so I had a flannel wash and changed into clean clothes for the first time. They'd see me till I got to Alston. I had two easy days ahead of me, I supposed. Not a bit of it though. I thought I'd nearly finished the Wall but there was another 4 miles of up and down and the gale was still blowing. Grey sky, no chance to charge my phone. I've texted Scharlie to say no battery and switched off my phone at 13%; enough for an emergency call if I need it. On the steep uphill stretches, my pace fell to a crawl. My legs were on autopilot and at times they just refused to move. Nothing for it but to plod on. It will be over eventually at

*Best preserved stretch of Hadrian's Wall just before Walltown*

the top of this slope. There are one or two very steep descents – the steps are slippy and I have to take extreme care not to slip and twist on ankle or worse.

The mind wanders. Maddie rang me yesterday to wish me luck and send her love. It was nice, when she hadn't wanted me to come in the first place. At the start of the lockdown she and Ruth had popped into Leveret Croft to say hello and bring us groceries. Maddie had been tearful saying she wanted me to meet my great-grandchildren. I'd been jocular at the time, now I did feel like dying. I can't believe that I am so tired and so slow. It must have really taken it out of me yesterday.

The last stretch of the wall, at a signaling turret with marvellous views in all directions, is most impressive. Only a metre or so high now, the Wall once stood 4 1/2 metres with a 1 1/2 m parapet – 20 feet, with a 12 foot deep valum ditch in front. All 77 miles built in only six years, all by hand. The quarry I camped in last night must have been where they cut stone. At Walltown, which I finally reached, there is another larger quarry. This is where Scharlie, Axel and I caught the bus back to Corbridge where we'd left the car in our three-day walk along the Wall. It seemed such a stroll then. Not so now. Maybe the weather, or the heavy pack or I'm that bit older.

I came upon Thirlwall Castle nestling next to a little stream. There was a

*Ruins of 12th-century Thirlwall Castle, Greenhead, built with stone from Hadrian's Wall*

large tape across the path up to the castle and a closed notice. Everything is closed. The notice said it was built in the 14th century during the border raids.

I crossed the main Newcastle-Carlisle railway line just north of Greenhead, making sure there was no train coming. Then I skirted round the golf course and sat under a pine tree and leant my back against it to rest. I stopped again a bit further on at a wooden bench. The route climbs through steep fields and then traverses right along a grassy road to an abandoned brick barn before slanting up the hillside to Blenkinsop common. There was little sign of a path and none at all on the common – hard going on grassy mounds heading for a trig point I could see on the horizon.

Checking the map I saw I needed to head to the left and then spotted a stile. The path headed due south across the vast Wain Rigg Common. No-one on the Way, no-one about all day. Just sheep and the occasional man walking a dog and a couple on the Wall bounding along at twice my pace. In the lush fields some ewes have 4-5 lambs, on the common, only one. Parts of the common must be very wet and boggy at certain times of the year; now it is just spongy after such a long dry spell. I reached farmland and climbed to the large farm at Upton. From there it was an easy walk to where I expected to stop. My shoulders were sore today, legs most tired. Good job it's a bank

*Crossing the main Newcastle-Carlisle (Tyne Valley) railway line, Greenhead*

holiday tomorrow and I'm getting to Alston in two days instead of trying to do it in one.

I spotted a green patch next to a tiny brook and planted my solar panel. The sun had just come out. I went to investigate and found an open patch lower down, thinking I might have to climb back up if there was no signal. In the event the signal, although weak, was strong enough. The intermittent sun was more cloud than shine. Never mind, I pitched camp. I was tired and tripped on a guy rope and nearly fell into the river!

Jon texted just now. I'm sitting next to Kellah Burn having made camp and managed to charge my phone. He said well done you did 22 miles yesterday.

This is an idyllic spot. Lying on my sleeping bag listening to the lambs and the crows. The ground is peppered with bright blue bugle flowers and as I write I can hear a woodpecker. Scharlie rang and told me about Dominic Cummings getting into trouble visiting his father in Durham and about wild campers causing fires in the Peak District and warned me that I might meet some animosity on my walk. I will need to be careful where I camp. I made supper and had a whole dehydrated meal – Thai rice chicken and peas – to

*Kellah Burn campsite in a bluebell dell*

give me energy. Perhaps I haven't been eating enough with only half a packet. I have half a spaghetti bolognese for tomorrow

I'm constantly amazed about how indefinite the path is at times. Quite unlike walking on the continent were there is a dab of paint every 3-4 m. Here the markers are spaced more than a mile apart. At most critical junctions there is a sign, but not always, and the fells and commons have few marker posts. This is still an adventure and a challenge. The white acorn signs that marked the Way are most welcome. These last few days have been hard, hard on my old body, but I feel good in myself as they say. You can see the history of the place, at least in a limited way, and feel how it ticks. And it's been interesting to be so alone and so in touch with this backbone of England. What a fascinating beautiful natural world, even if so man-made.

*One of the clearer sections of the walk on Blenkinsop Common and Wain Rigg*

# Day 6: Kellah Burn to Gilderdale Burn, Alston

**Monday 25 May 2020  9.1km, 5.7 miles**

I woke at 7.30 with the sun popping over the trees of my sylvan glade. It's totally idyllic to wake to birdsong, bubbling burn, blue sky and, best of all, no wind! I make a can of tea and watch a vole popping in and out of the grass on the other side of the brook. I saw two yesterday on the common. They must be easy to spot by an eagle-eyed hawk if I can see them. There were owls in the night, two different calls, one the usual two-whit note of the tawny owl and the other a long drawn out single tone of a long-eared owl.

It would be good to have more sugar for my tea, but I don't really miss my usual creature comforts – the news, Netflix, email and the routine of modern life. I look at my gypsy encampment and think of life as a hobo. How do they keep going. I've only done a week in May before I need a fuel dump in Alston.

On the Wall, yesterday, a young couple were bounding towards me on a line above me on the wall top were I should have been but had missed

*Lazy start washing and sorting gear, Kellah Burn*

the path momentarily. And I was crawling along. He was in shorts, as I was, and I thought about the Romans in their leather shorts and sandals. What a practical outfit for most weathers and climes of their empire. Cold perhaps in winter on this their most northerly border. No doubt they had that sorted like much else. What an example of fortitude, ingenuity, vision and persistence the Wall and all their endeavours provide. Yet, since very young when I first learned about their conquests, I have rather rejected their system and ideals. I liked Latin at first, then refused to learn it and switched to woodwork. It would have been important to learn 2000 years ago, even 100 as a lawyer. But today? Now I regret not persisting. I'd have preferred to have been a Barbarian than a Roman. Even on the losing side. Yet my whole life has been about deskwork – writing, analysing. That seems more Roman than Barbarian. We obviously admire those civilisations that wrote about themselves. Archaeology tells us such an impoverished tale about those that didn't. But the complex detail of daily life, how people lived, what they thought, what they believed in eludes us in the same way it is impossible for me to convey the detail of this journey. The minute actions to stay alive and well, the thoughts and feelings one experiences with such a prolonged aloneness. It's not just that I'm alone on this walk, because of Covid all is different. To breakfast and pack. There

*Hartley Burn, where I'd meant to camp*

are bluebells bright in the sun on the hillside opposite. Such a delightfully, lazy morning sorting gear, charging phone, washing feet, packing.

Scharlie phoned and told me it was better to take the South Tyne Way rather than the Pennine Way but I can't see it on the map. I guess it will become clear. Apart from thinking about aches and pains, fantasising about calling a taxi or taking a bus to ride between towns, one's main preoccupation is navigation. The way is sparsely marked, which is good of course. But in the wind it is impossible at times to get the map out. And then, since the Way is a contrived path, it isn't always obvious or as well trodden as the ancient trackways which cross and recross the hillsides everywhere. I'm pleased and amazed how unspoiled it is after all I'd heard. The clouds are moving fast so there must be a breeze today even if it's sheltered in my little dell. As I rise the wind picks up and blows along the stream chilling me in my cotton T-shirt. A gentle lethargy sweeps over me and I could sit here all day. I need to move. Pity I'm not walking north with the sun on my back, as I'd be able to charge my phone as I walked.

So no more Strava. It's back to the traditional map and compass that I'm used to. I'm writing this near the end of the Maiden Way, my only companion the curlew and lapwing, rabbits and hare. If I wasn't so tired this day would be

*Ruined barn, Dodd's Rigg, Hartley Burn*

delightful. What am I saying, it is delightful. As I walk I startle up lapwing and their alarm call startles young lambs and pipits. I love the bubbling call of the curlew. A pair circle back and forth over me in the strong breeze and land like airliners. Curlew and lapwing look so big and majestic on the wing and so small and defenceless on the ground. Pairs of golden plover make a lot of noise and display to draw me away from their nests.

At the A689 motorbikes and fast cars with spoilers, their engines tuned for higher speeds, mistiming; men on racing bikes. None stopped, as I did constantly, to marvel at the magical flight of the circling birds. Rabbits ran out from under my feet and scampered for their warren in a sandy hollow. The Maiden Way, along which this part of the Pennine Way runs, is a Roman road. I thought again about the Romans. They walked; from Hadrian's Wall to Rome, some of them, and on into Asia. Didn't think anything of 20 miles a day. Perhaps not the 74-year-olds! I wonder how they crossed the Alps. Hannibal crossing with elephants. Defeated, but his name remembered. How many Roman emperors could I name after Hadrian – Tiberius, Julius Caesar, Claudius, Marcus Aurelius and Augustus of course and the infamous Draco and Caligula. How the mind wanders. I've taken off my boots to give my weary sore feet a rest. No blisters, but sore joints.

*Lapwing luring me away from its nest on Maiden Way*

On the A689 there is a short terrace of houses with a large St George's flag bravely flying in the wind and three burly men in t-shirts chatting outside. I wondered, as I crossed the road enjoying the song of the curlew, if they went shooting. And just then I saw line of butts winding uphill. A lapwing swooped low in front of me. I had never noticed the orange tipped wings before. The first burn I come to, Thinhope Burn, is delightful – clear abundant water. But it is right next to the road. At Glendew Burn, which Scharlie had mentioned, the manicured lawns of Knarsdale Hall are spotted with Magnolia and tea roses looking pretty against the viaduct.

I had to decide whether to continue along the traditional way or take the South Tyne Way along the old railway line. I fancied a little walking on the flat so I climbed the path at the end of the viaduct I'd spotted from high up on the hillside. Just a few miles more. There was a chill wind when I stopped and there had been a strong breeze most of the day but I expect I'll miss it when it's still and I'm roasting.

I met a young farmer on a quad bike in a field full of sheep with lambs. He asked me if I was doing the Way and I said, Yes, I know I'm not supposed to.

It doesn't bother me he said. Have you come from the Northumbrian hills.

From Kirk Yetholm, or as near as I could get without going into Scotland.

*Viaduct at Knarsdale Hall, Glendew Burn*

Yes, we don't want to go into Scotland at all. You'll be camping then, you'll have a tent.

I thought I'd camp on the burn below Whitley Castle.

Yes that would do.

A couple of dozen lambs were playing king of the castle on a small mound next the farmhouse. They look healthy I said.

Not that one, it looks drunk, he said pointing to a lamb wobbly on its feet.

This Covid is like foot and mouth for humans.

It must have been bad for you.

Yes it was. Closed us down for a year. Still have restrictions. If you bring a new animal in you have to quarantine it for six days. But this is bad and people are dying and all.

It was a day of poor navigation. I went wrong from the start since I wasn't camped where I planned at Hartley Burn, but higher up next to its tributary Kellah Burn. This was fortunate since the glade I camped in was secluded and beautiful whereas where I had intended to camp turned out to be a huge meadow and much more exposed. I went wrong again at the A689 and if I'd turned over the map and looked at the next stage of the way, I'd have realised. But I'd made it to where I planned to camp – Gilderdale, the burn below the

*Covered market cross, Alston, where I ate my grapes and scones out of the rain*

Roman fort at Whitley Castle.

The campsite is another idyllic spot sheltered behind a wall with a stone to sit on next to a babbling burn. I pitch camp and Scharlie rings asking for help getting on to zoom for her HVCA meeting. Already that all seems a long way away. Such a while without any creature comforts, outside all the time, no sofa and TV, soft bed, not a chair, nor a roof of course. And it's only been 6 days.

*Gilderdale Burn where I pitched camp in the corner of the walls*

# Pennine Way Central

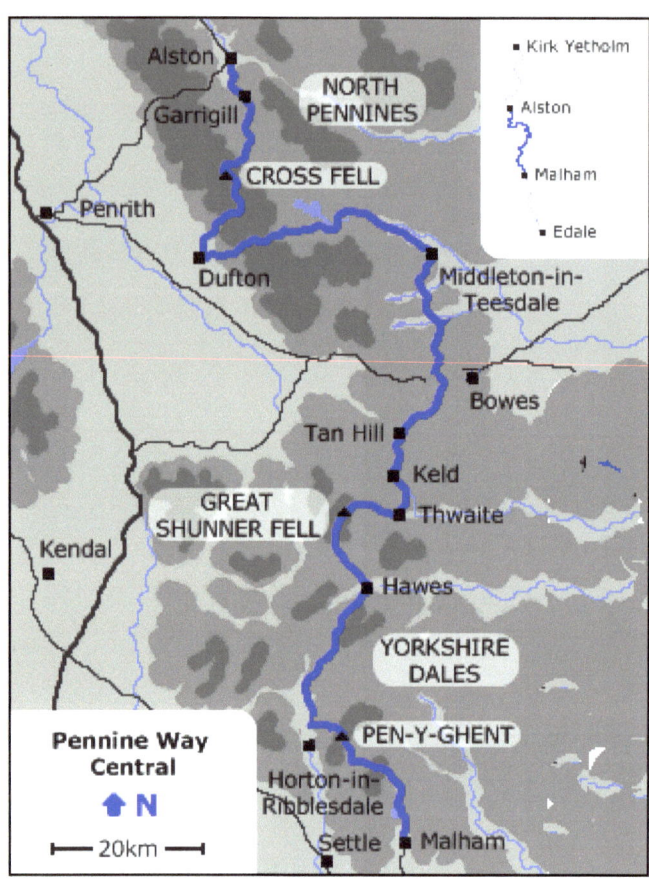

# Day 7: Gilderdale Burn to Cash Burn, Garrigill

**Tuesday 26 May 2020  26.4km, 16.4 miles**

I'm lying beside the South Tyne River where it falls over a shelf of rock. I stopped for lunch and had a sleep in the sun for an hour. This morning I woke at 6.30 and a pair of heron flew off the burn and sailed away as I emerged from the tent. The usual breakfast ablutions and packing and I was away by 7.30. A climb out of the ravine and an easy walk into Alston.

I arrived at the post office at 9.05 to find it didn't open until 10. But the nice woman gave me the poste-restante box Ghazala had posted a week earlier, so I had a leisurely hour to transfer the new food and clean clothes to my sack and the dirty washing in bits and bobs to the box, which I relabelled. It was drizzling so I took the orange, grapes and scones I'd bought in the Co-op to the roofed market cross. Alston is charming with steep narrow streets and an air of the sixties. Pity that everywhere is closed, I could do with a coffee. At 10 there was a little queue at the post office so I had to wait a few minutes

*Covered market cross, Alston, where I ate my grapes and scones out of the rain*

*Post office, Alston, where I collected my first poste-restante box*

*Bridge at Alston where I stopped out of the rain*

before posting the box back home. I climbed the hill to the end of the village to see if the bakery was open, but no joy; only a delightful Quaker meeting house. I bought a pasty at the Spar in the garage and a lighter to replace the one that had failed.

I ate half the pasty under the bridge out of the rain before setting off along the river walk. Easy, flat walking. Drizzling a little, but it soon cleared and I stopped to change into shorts. There are isolated sheep farms dotted along the way. At Bleagate, where the Tyne curves east, I stopped in the shade to get out the suntan cream and my cap. As I emerged from the shade I saw a figure in the garden, stock still, with a black featureless head. I looked again and saw it was a woman in a grey dress wearing a beekeeping mask. I raise my hand in greeting. She didn't move. Then I saw her husband working his vegetable patch and said hi and they both said hello. I wish I'd stopped and chatted, but I was shaken by the strange sight.

Along the river a mother mallard crossed the path leading her ducklings to the water for the first time. I startled them and mum flapped downstream then back making a great commotion to distract me just like the flocks of lapwing. Almost into Garrigill, where I stopped for lunch by the river, I saw a young stag crossing. I stood as still as I could and watched it tiptoeing across the rocks

*Young stag crossing the rapids on the South Tyne River*

through the rapids. It took flight as soon as I raised my camera and shot away downstream.

A young woman and two children came past as I was packing and said hello. I met them again on the road into Garrigill. She said they lived at Leadgate. Her husband was doing a roof at Tyne Head and they were walking to meet him. They were imagining they were on holiday and walking along the beach.

How far is your walk, the boy asked.

270 miles.

It will take you a couple of days then.

20, I said.

You're wife will miss you, he said.

That's why I've got a solar panel on my pack.

There's a good signal at Tyne Head, he said.

Garrigill is a pretty village and I was tempted to stop but pressed on, going past the turnoff at a house with a small wind turbine and going back to check and seeing the sign hidden in the hedge.

It's a long arduous stony road, widened recently. This looks to be a huge shooting estate - all new fences and a man repairing the stone walls. I said

*Garrigill*

hello. Grand day.

Yes it's fine, he said.

There was a sign saying the landowner had withdrawn access to the land outside the right-of-way and another saying how important burning the heather, draining the moors and trapping predators were for protecting endangered species of ground nesting birds and what a good job of carbon capture the peat bogs did. I thought how without driven grouse shooting the moors would be treed and would support a much more complex web of life. Not only that they would capture more carbon, control rain water run-off and prevent flash floods.

The road was as wide as two carriageways and went on and on. Scharlie had been reading the guide and said it was called the Corpse Road. Well named I thought. Where were they were taking the corpses, I wondered. (I later learnt the road went from Garrigill to consecrated ground at Kirkland Church at a distance of over 10 miles rising to 2,576 feet on the northern flank of Cross Fell).

A cyclist passed me coming down. It looked like a hybrid bike, rather than a full mountain bike, and it had an old-fashioned saddlebag, the like of which I hadn't seen for years. I was impressed. I was just thinking I'd only seen a couple

*Camp at Cash Burn*

of grouse when, as I neared Cash Burn, where I intended to stop, two mother grouse with a pair of chicks ran out of the heather in front of me. Maybe they don't fly this time of the year because of the chicks.

It's a lovely evening – a light breeze and a clear blue sky with birdsong. My phone is all charged so I rang Scharlie and told her I'd arrived and I will stay here the night. The burn was narrower here but running well and, although exposed to the wind, the site was good and the wind was light. I pitched camp and settled down to boil water for dinner. I poured boiling water into the dehydrated pack of Thai chicken and put the pan down to seal the bag. The pan tipped, I grabbed and the boiling tea water splashed on my heel. I took off my sock, doused it in cold water, got out the first aid kit and smothered the scald in antiseptic cream. It didn't hurt at first but is now very tender. I hope it's all right in my boot tomorrow. What an idiot; I'll never learn. So many things to keep track of, and things can go wrong so easily when you're tired. Still it's been a good day and I'm feeling stronger. The pack is a burden but my legs felt okay today and the last two days have seemed much easier since the wind died down.

Greg's Hut, mountain refuge

# Day 8: Cash Burn to Cauldron Snout

**Wednesday 27 May 2020  33.9km, 21.1 miles**

It was a good night, light breeze although cold again. A bird, maybe a Little Owl, kept up a peeping note all night. I woke about 5 but it was too cold to move until 5.30 when the sun began peeping over the shoulder of the fell. I put out the solar panel and fetched water for tea. I was more careful this time and got away without mishap.

It's a long haul to Greg's Hut and I wondered for a moment if I'd missed my way. The bothy is well appointed with two rooms and a porch for coal. There is a sitting room with a dozen plastic chairs and a steel table for cooking on with camping stoves and a second room with a stove and sleeping platform for about 8 to 10 people. There is water from a pipe 20 metres away and a solitary tree in its own walled garden.

From here the path becomes a proper mountain track, indistinct at times. It also takes a sudden change in direction half a mile

*Stove and sleeping platform, Greg's Hut*

*Summit of Cross Fell*

*Radio station Great Dun Fell*

beyond the hut, which must catch out the unwary as the main path continues straight on. It's not very steep and I plod on, reaching the top about 9. There is a huge beehive shaped shelter with quadrant arms so you can shelter in any wind direction. There was a solitary camper emerging from his tent a hundred yards away on the lee side of the hill. I waved, he waved. Up late I thought, but a lot faster than me I bet. The next section is an easy stroll in this weather. In the mist or bad weather these tops could be more serious.

I passed the cairn on Little Dun Fell and headed up to the white geodesic dome on the top of Great Dun. I don't know what it is, but I bet it's a lot more than a weather station. (It is, in fact, a radar station and part of the air traffic control system). There were half a dozen cars and a similar number of workers and a solitary cyclist. He whizzed off downhill, disappearing in seconds.

Steve Snow rang on Knock Fell to talk about our renewable energy proposal. I was following a bright green track and not concentrating on route finding. When he rang off I realised I'd gone wrong on the top of Green Fell trending to the east. Luckily I could see a large cairn on the skyline to my right and headed out across the broken rocks of the Curricks. From there it was easy and there were stone markers with chiseled arrows as far as Swindale Beck where I stopped for lunch and made coffee.

*Ancient clapper bridge over Great Rundale Beck*

It seemed a long way to Dufton through pretty farmland with flowering elder alive with buzzing bees. It had been cloudy and cool, but now the sun came out and I was glad to see a spreading beech tree with a shady bench at the head of the village. I stopped and took off my boots. The shops and services were at the other end of the village. I didn't think I had the energy to go and see. I needed to wait till the heat of the day went before attempting the climb up to Maize Beck where I planned to camp. I've left the watershed of the Tyne and have entered the headwaters of the Tees.

I spent two or three hours lounging about. An old boy of about 80 came past and said hello. He was limping with arthritis. That's the best bit, he said, looking at me sitting on the grass in the shade of a wall, writing.

Like my father used to say when I came back from climbing expeditions, it must be great when it's over.

On his way back I asked him if there was a pump or a tap in the village. I'll give you water, he said. I followed him to his house and he filled my 2 L bottle. I could make tea. He came out again to collect wood for his stove.

It's handy having a timber yard next door, he said. I keep a tally and settle up later. They make wooden hay rakes; maybe one of the last makers in England.

*Shady tree were I rested in Dufton*

Every village used to have one.

Do they use ash?

Yes, they used to use ramin but can't get it any more. His great-grandfather started the business.

What else is Dufton famous for?

Nothing really. It's one of a string of fell edge villages on the edge of the moor. It's vast the moor. You'll see when you cross.

Yes I saw coming over Cross Fell. Have you always lived here?

No, can't you tell my Cornish accent. We came here hillwalking and came to live here 40 years ago.

Later when I was packing, he came out with a plate of fruit – an apple and three oranges. Would you like some, he said. I remember fruit was always the problem on a long walk.

I could murder an Apple.

Take them all. It's very generous of you. Think nothing of it. I ate two of the oranges and they were delicious. As I was shouldering my pack I nodded to the woman whose young girls had been playing on bikes around the tree.

You'll be off then?

Yes. Must have been difficult these last weeks with the children off school.

*Tree stump in Dufton*

We're lucky here, and with the weather, they can play outside. Would you like a sandwich to take with you?

I'm fine. Thank you.

I can do you one with ham or cheese.

How about a small one of ham and cheese?

You're really going for it.

A while later she brought out a blue plastic bag. I've made a bag like my mother would have. You can have the yoghurt tonight.

Thank you that's very kind. By the way what's the nice gentleman's name?

Ron.

And yours?

Jane.

Thank you Jane, stay safe.

At the end of the village, just before the path diverted uphill, there was a bench and a rubbish bin. I stopped and opened the bag. The sandwiches were on brown bread. It tasted good. I ate one and saved one for later and the malt loaf. I ate the yoghurt and the chocolate bar.

I was setting off quite late but thought I could make it to Maize Beck. You climb a tarmac road at first. It was still hot and I put a handkerchief under my

*Dufton House*

cap to protect my neck. I was going slowly but fairly steadily. A couple passed me going down and we chatted. They came walking from Yorkshire. I had just started up the steep path when Scharlie rang saying she had lost her phone and couldn't open the barn door to look for it. I had just dropped my pants with a call of nature and it was difficult juggling the phone and my shorts.

I thought of stopping near Hannah's Well. There was a sheltered spot, water and the signal the three essentials. But I thought I'd press on as planned. A bit of a mistake. The path divided into two branches at the majestic High Cup Nick and I rang Scharlie to check the guide. But I lost signal and decided to take the one that looked shorter.

I came to a bridge across the beck and again wanted to know whether to cross to the North side, but again no signal. There was a place to camp but I knew Scharlie would be worried. So I opted to press on, crossing over to the north side since the map showed this to be the better route and I would need to be on that side later. I reasoned I would get a signal soon and pressed on. It was about 8 and the sun was still bright. There must be a signal at Birkdale Farm, I thought. I got there soon after 9.30, but still no signal. I was going well by now. The adrenaline had kicked in and because it was flat I could stride out.

Someone came to the door to see why the dogs were barking. He saw me

*Harthwaite on start of path to High Cup Nick*

*High Cup Nick*

*Maize Beck*

and went back in. Hello I shouted. He came out again.

What you want?

Have you got a telephone? I want to ring my wife and tell her I'm all right.

No telephone here.

I didn't think so. When do you get a signal?

Which way are you going? I indicated with my stick. Just above the head of the dam, he said.

I checked the map – mile or so more. I pressed on and reached Cow Green Reservoir dam as it was getting dark just before 10. No signal at the dam but a place to camp. So I quickly changed out of my boots into Clogs and put up the tent and sorted the gear. With my warm clothes on I headed half a mile or so up the road. Finally the phone beeped and I rang Scharlie and texted my beacon position. I made tea and ate the sandwich and buttered malt loaf. See if I can write and thank Jane and Ron, I thought. Maybe I can write a letter to Cornish Ron and his neighbour, Jane, at Townend Dufton. (Back home I managed to get his address and post him a copy of my journal. You made an old man very happy, he texted, remembering when I did it years ago.) The noise of the water crashing down the Cauldron Snout by the side of the tent didn't wake me.

*Bridge across to north side of Maize Beck*

# Day 9: Cauldron Snout to Holwich, Teeside

**Thursday 28 May 2020  14.5km, 9.0 miles**

I awoke at 5 and went back to sleep till 6. I had a proper wash in the river, taking care not to slip on the rocks and get swept down into the rapids. A leisurely start, drying the tent, packing, charging phone and writing journal. Away soon after 8.30.

Because the rock has little friction the descent by the side of the waterfalls is tricky. It would be easy to slip and sprain an ankle. I was feeling stiff from yesterday so I took it easy. The walk along the riverbank begins well with a grassy path but soon turns into a scramble through the boulder field below Falcon Crags. Curlew and bright white gulls wheel above the river below the crags. My toe was hurting so I stopped, took out the first aid kit and removed my boots and socks. Sure enough I had a blister on the second to the smallest toe. I rummaged through my quite comprehensive kit and found one of the small Compeed plasters Ghazala had given me. Further on I slipped on a

*Cauldron Snout, the roiling outflow from Cow Green Reservoir*

stone near the water and my foot flopped in and wetted my socks. Not badly, fortunately. I checked and they were not totally soaked.

At the point where the river bends south the path climbs to Sawyer Hill. There is a simple bench dedicated to Albert Craddock "who loved this place" and Margaret Gibson "Blithe spirit". I wondered about a bench for Scharlie and me when we're gone. Somewhere on the Derbyshire stretch of the Pennine Way, and thought about writing something in my will. Just after the bridge at Sawyer Hill there was an elderly couple making tea on the other side of the river. They had a sturdy frame tent and chairs and quite a campsite, all towed behind a big red motorcycle. I shouted hello.

Not many about. You're the first walker we've seen.

You get a lot on that bike.

It's a big one.

I ride BMW 100RS.

We had a 70R.

A nice bike. Like a sewing machine.

The path rejoins the river and re-crosses at a bridge. There is a pull up the hill at Cronkley. Nothing normally, but when you're tired the mind runs on imagining itself at the next stopping place, the lunch spot, the planned

*Boulder field below Falcon Crags; most tedious to get over*

campsite, and the next settlement. It seems so close in the imagination. Then you look at the map and realise all the detail you've missed and how it's much further. And then you walk and the distance and the detail magnifies again, almost overwhelmingly so at times. But you go on placing one foot in front of the other.

It's a startlingly beautiful day and I should be enjoying it more. I am enjoying it, but I'm tired and achy from yesterday and it's getting hot and I'm worried it will get hotter. I meet a couple coming the other way and step aside for them at a little bridge.

We're doing the Tees Way. We left the car at the end.

I'm doing the Pennine.

Good for you. Got a tent then? Marvellous weather for it.

A bit hot.

Can't complain

I press on, past the quarry with its rusty processing towers, past Bleabeck Force and finally reach High Force on the Tees, a 70-foot waterfall, yet I can't see it despite my best efforts risking life and limb leaning out on a tree. I stop in the shade of a birch and have lunch and write my journal. It's chilly in the welcome shade. I carve thin slices of lomo, like prosciutto ham, and eat them

*Quarry near Bleabeck Force*

with thin slices of tart green apple that Ron gave me yesterday. Delicious. I'd had the last orange for breakfast.

After an hour or so at about 2:30 I decided to make a move to Low Force and beyond to get away from the crowds. So I do my pack and set off with my blue handkerchief under my cap. I try and give the hordes of people coming along the path a good berth and have to climb off the path and wait at times.

Low Force is even busier, because you can get to the water. Young men jump off high rocks or the metal bridge over the river doing somersaults to impress. I'm impressed. There are loads of families sunbathing and groups of young mums with toddlers. Good job the virus doesn't do so well outdoors.

I've been planning to go on past Middleton, after a tea break, and walk in the cool of the evening. But I'm tired after yesterday and when I come to a grassy corner under a tree next to the river with a stone to sit on and a signal I decide to stop and make tea and contemplate spending the night here. If I get an early night I can make a dawn start and do a lot more before noon and the afternoon heat.

I get the new map out. Nearly half way and onto the southern map tomorrow! There are two full pages to Hawes. Either go fast and try and do them in two days and collect my box on Saturday or go at a leisurely pace

*High Force, biggest waterfall in Britain*

and collect on Monday. It's a pity how the days have fallen. It's partly because I'm faster or go further each day than I calculated and partly because of the bank holiday last Monday, which was nice and gave me two relatively easy days after the big day from Bellingham. I checked online and the post office in Hawes closes at 12.30 on Saturday. I could never make it by midday so I can take it easy over the next three days. I got out the Thermarest and dozed then slept for an hour and at 6 I decided no one was about so I put up the tent. I cooked a full pack of the Thai green curry. Up to now I've been managing with half a packet. Perhaps I haven't been eating enough. The full pack is 800 K calories. But then I've been supplementing that with the occasional pasty and the sandwiches yesterday. Not to mention my oat nut breakfast and oat bars during the day.

I was just congratulating myself when I heard a woman's voice. Hello there, excuse me! I didn't turn round. Then I saw a blue Land Rover going through the gate behind me. Where on earth had she come from. I expect her husband will be out in a while to tell me to be off. It's 7 o'clock and I'm ready for an early bed! We are now in the land of becks not burns, dales not glens, fells and not moors. Becks, dales, fells, all Viking words as is the word force from the Danish foss for waterfall.

*Camp next to the River Tees, near Low Way Farm*

# Day 10: Holwich to God's Bridge

**Friday 29 May 2020  20.8km, 12.9 miles**

I woke at 5 or so feeling refreshed and did my things. No bother from the woman last night. It was a mystery how she'd been there at all in a Land Rover since you can't drive along the river and the only way was from the field in and out of the same gate. The way winds through endless flower meadows. All along the fell edge, between the moor and the river, there are hay meadows and barns. No wonder Ron mentioned hay rakes. Haymaking must have been a big event each year – essential for life and cash.

The soil is sandy and as I walk I startle dozens of rabbits. There are mallard swimming against the strong current. Birdsong. Already it's getting hot and I can feel the heat of the newly risen sun. The path climbs away from the river for a good while and as I descend I see flashes of silver through the trees. The Tees is already much wider. Two black and white birds have been tracking my course. (Later I pealise they are Oyster Catchers.) Finally the herd of cows

*Meadows and fell edge farms and barns along River Tees below Crossthwaite Common*

this place was made for, 7 to 8 mums with calves, bellowing as they plunge and splash across a little beck.

An old barn, it's roof missing tiles, broken panes of glass in the windows, still packed with straw. A bubbling beck. This is a mesmerisingly magical morning.

Nearing this top of Harter Fell, a copse of trees, a dead rabbit, a murder of crows on the skyline, curlew calling. More dead rabbits and the crows patrolling the edge, chased by a Lapwing pair. How on earth do these birds rear their young?

I stop for coffee in the meagre shade of a stonewall. The sun is too high to offer much shade. The two reservoirs look low. I can see the plantation I need to pass and the fell beyond, rolling rather than steep. I lean across the cool stone of the wall while my coffee cools, laying my arm along the rock, feeling the cold of the previous night.

At Grassholme Farm a portly farmer with a grey monks tonsure greets me.
How far are you going?
All the way.
From Kirk Yetholm?
Yes or very near.
We can go into Scotland. We go all the time. My son is in Stirling now. They

*Barn, Eel Beck*

rang wanting some beef and we found them for them. I'm a livestock buyer. I was in Cumbria and the police stopped me. I said I'm buying livestock. I have a letter. Don't worry we can see this as a farm vehicle, they said.

What county are we in here?

It used to be North Yorkshire. It's County Durham now.

Is your wife alive still?

Oh yes. She's off on a delivery with our daughter. Can't see our grandchild though. My other daughter's husband shielding.

What's your name?

Richard Sayer, like it says on the trailer – Sawyer Livestock. There were a lot of youngsters at the reservoir slipway yesterday. They had to chain it up.

There were lots at Low Force – it was like Blackpool. Can I get water at the reservoir?

No, but I'll fill your bottle for you. Lots of people used to do the walk, lots of older people. It was like a motorway the year before last.

It's great now I like the solitude. Keep safe.

The men had just finished mowing at the dam and were having a smoke on the picnic table in the reservoir car park. They passed me on the hill climb in their van. Looking back the old pack bridge was exposed looking forlorn in a

*Old packhorse bridge in a sea of mud at Grassholme Reservoir*

sea of mud.

I got a bit lost going through the fields of Hunderthwaite Moor. There were two wallers and I waved at them and headed off. I was on the right track but doubted myself. I convinced myself I should be further left. I could see a yellow marker on a gate in the far distance and headed for it even though I felt the path should be heading for the coll at the lowest point of the ridge. When I got there it was yellow string. So I climbed to the ridge and headed right to strike the path. There were two mountain bikers heading down the way I should have come and I got back on track.

I continued across the moor and dropped down to Blackton Reservoir. At the farm at High Birk Hat there was a National Trust visitor centre celebrating Hannah Hauxwell's meadow. The meadow didn't look that special compared with those along the Tees earlier this morning or even Leveret Croft. But when I read about her later and watched a documentary by Barry Cockcroft on Youtube I realised what an exceptional life she'd led, living alone with her beloved cows, surviving through harsh winters, fetching water for them from the frozen reservoir and carrying bales of hay on her back up the snow covered fields. At Low Birk Hat, where Hannah had lived, there was a picnic bench and I stopped for lunch. The farm is now a smart home; quite different

*Hannah Hauxwell, Low Birk Hatt Farm, Baldersdale, 1989*

from the bleak house in the film. It was pleasant in the shade of the trees. The only catch was that a young man was strimming. Obviously not heard of Scharlie's wild gardening.

I thought to collect water at the reservoir spillway but the map showed good becks at Deepdale River, the River Greeta and Sleightholme Beck. I had enough to get me there, and enough to last the night in an emergency. The walking was pleasant enough over Brown Rigg Moss. A trackway had been built across the fell to Race Yate. I wondered if indeed there was an annual race here and this track was to get cars up to the moor top. I imagine it as a famous Durham fell race.

The beck was dry where I planned to stop, so I pressed on across the moors with the usual complement of curlew and plover to Ravock Castle – a cairn marking the spot and dropped down to the noisy A66. I was wondering how to cross when I came to the sign saying underpass 200 m.

After a bit of a wander off course I found God's Bridge, the natural tunnel formed in the limestone that provides a perfect bridge. Not that it is necessary today, since the River Greeta wasn't flowing. What to do, no water! Nevertheless I decided I'd stop here, so I left my pack and walked back to the house 100 yards up the field and asked the woman if she could let me

*God's Bridge, natural limestone bridge over River Greeta*

have some water.

Would it be all right if I camped here?

It's not our field, so it's not for me to say. There are cows.

They shouldn't bother me.

There was a shallow pool under the bridge and I went down to bathe my sore feet. A duckling was swimming about, seemingly oblivious to my presence. It came within a few feet, diving under feeding. I was just sorting myself out when the woman's husband arrived – a pleasant, tall young man with a can of beer in his hand.

Straight from the fridge he said, handing it to me. We chatted. He worked in a local farm, with sheep.

Did you see the duck?

The young mallard?

Yes, it's the children's pet. They found it abandoned as a chick. They tried to find its parents then my boy had it in his bedroom a couple of weeks feeding it ground up chicken pellets. I didn't think it would survive but it did. Now it comes up to the house each night on its own and goes into a box in the garden.

He asked me if I was retired and how I was finding the walk. We talked

*I camped on the grass in front of the buttress of dismantled railway abutment*

about New Zealand. He'd been there with his wife, a teacher, and they had thought of emigrating. But the kids came and we have things to do to the house and on the farm. Now it's too late, they only want young ones.

I pitch camped, opened the can and cooked. The beer went to my head. I rang Scharlie. The two children came down to the pool, the boy with a can of beer, his sister with food for the duckling. I thought of the glossy mallard drake I'd seen dead in the grass on the moor above the A66.

*Notice showing next leg of journey across Bowes Moor*

# Day 11: God's Bridge to Keld

**Saturday 30 May 2020  17.2 km, 10.7 miles**

I awake feeling somewhat downcast. My little toe was worse as was the chaffing between my buttocks. Maybe it was the little alcohol that had gone to my head last night or maybe I just had enough of it all. It felt like I'd finished, even though I still had nearly halfway to go. I did what I could with my minor injuries and dressed in a fresh set of clothes. I was drinking my tea, watching the duckling come out of the water to preen herself in the sun when a skein of 21 geese flew over honking like mad in their V formation with a following group of three and a single straggler trying to keep up. It lifted my spirits.

From God's Bridge the grassy path climbs to the moor. I walked accompanied by the usual bevy of pirouetting peewits (lapwing). A startled grouse flew from under my feet leaving her chick scuttling along the path. I stepped left and expect they were reunited soon after. It happened again five minutes later, this time a pheasant mum and two chicks. Mum ran and didn't take flight.

*Tricky descent to Sleightholme Beck*

The path reached the Sleightholme Beck and followed it all along the crest of a deep ravine. A kestrel flew from trees on the cliff below me mobbed by a female blackbird. There is a steep and nasty descent to the bridge across the beck. The path is narrow and green again. Nothing and no one as far as the eye can see in all directions. Only shooting butts. I realise I have become habituated to the solitude and find it normal.

On reaching the metal road a field barn has been renovated as a second home. It looked nice but has few small windows on the three sides I could see. I expect they have a big picture window where the door used to be. You pass Sleightholme Farm and a gate with a notice saying, road unsuitable for vehicles. This is grouse shooting territory and the road is fine. It would be nice to drive it one day.

Where the way leaves the road there are a line of simple wooden boxes, rather like three-sided timber compost bins, with painted numbers. Perhaps they have found that the crude butts are just as effective in disguising shooters from the startled alarmed birds as the stone turf ones I've seen earlier or the line of stone butts next to the river below. In August through to December I expect the beck is renamed Slaughterholme. Scharlie rang to warn me about mineshafts on Tan Hill and not to leave the path

*Sleightholme Moor, mercifully dry, but bound to be boggy in wet weather*

A female grouse and a covey of half a dozen young fly up from the path in front of me and the young ones scatter while mum stands her ground to one side of the path until I get near. Beds of dancing cotton grass, sunshine, wind. The walking becomes more difficult. This must be boggy at other times. All this is peat. I guess trees would set seed in sheltered spots if there were no sheep. I passed two stone walled pens. They didn't look in use and there are not that many sheep. Grouse are the cash crop now.

There was good water in Frumming Beck and I can hear it bubbling over the rocks. With a name like frumming one might have expected more of a torrent, but the moor is very flat and the incline gentle. An engine noise, then a succession of motorbikes on the thin line of the road confirming that what I thought might be a roof on the skyline was in fact the Tan Hill, the highest pub in Britain (528m) and where I'll stop for coffee.

The path is most indistinct here and would normally be very wet. Is this what they call flow country! Shots! What I wonder are they shooting? I've been hearing it on and off all the way across the moor. Now I'm nearer what I thought on the skyline was the roof but is in fact a rocky outcrop. But the roof is right next to it.

There are a few bikers at the inn and although there was a picnic table it was

*Tan Hill Inn - highest pub in Britain (528 m). Bikers to the left, boy racers to the right*

facing the road in a car park full of machinery. So I climbed the rocks next to the pub and found a spot out of the wind to make coffee and have a rest. I'm getting sick of the meat, great as it is, and just had an oat bar. I vow to buy some Parmesan in Hawes if I can and send the final piece of lomo back in the box.

By the time I came back to the inn to resume my walk there were dozens of motorbikes and fast cars and lots of young men talking and fooling around – the bikers all in black leather in one car park and the boy racers in T-shirts in the other. Time to leave.

The path that starts as a grouse shooters road quickly becomes a green path. There is a breeze and strong sun and it is pleasant walking. I can see signs of mine workings, dips on the ground near the path and gouging in the valley sides, with veins of black coal showing. I passed through a gate near some workings from Durham into Yorkshire – the Yorkshire Dales National Park in fact.

I stop at Lad's Gill and strip off, thinking this must be as lonely as it gets and doze off. I had just washed and dressed when a mountain biker popped over the ridge and pedalled past. Covid seems to given mountain bikers a dispensation to go anywhere and footpaths are no longer sacrosanct. Having said that, this may well be a bridle path, which reminds me, I'd like to bring

*Lad's Gill where I stopped for a sleep on the soft grass*

my bike up here.

Seven stone barns where the moor meets the pasture – so crucial in the past to get through a harsh winter. An eyeless abandoned farmhouse. A barn with the door ajar, held by a rock.

Inside a small room; it looks as though a sheep could have given birth here. I undid the latch on the door to the two-storey part and stepped into the past. Filled with sweet smelling small bales of hay the mezzanine stocked full. Hard to imagine how the small pastures in the valley bottom produced enough hay to fill up all the barns in the valley. How did the economy work? How does it work now?

I looked down on Keld, full of cars and no sign of a shop. I stopped at the force on East Gill, an idyllic spot with people picnicking. There were two benches for walkers and I found a tree for shade. I'm thinking to stop here, but there's no signal; probably have to climb high to get one. So I stop awhile. It's only 4 o'clock. Maybe everyone will disappear soon and leave the place in peace and I can camp. The only problem is the lack of signal and texting to say I am in Keld and okay. I had an idea. I could ask someone to ring her when they got home. Three people went past looking like serious walkers so I said hello and explained. They said they would. They asked me if I was doing the

*Tiny pastures and stone barns Startindale Gill, above Keld*

whole thing and how I found it. I said despite all the stories I'd heard it was a marvellous walk and had shown me parts of England I didn't know. Of course I've been lucky with the weather. In heavy rain and mud it wouldn't be much fun. I thought of the passage today across Bowes Moor where there are no slabs and only a few wooden bridges with drainage channels. It's like a huge flat sponge and must get very wet.

A couple stopped and asked the way to Kidson force. I checked my map and suggested they continue on the other side of the river on the Swale trail. The way drops down to Keld from here and goes along the riverbank. They asked me if I was camping and if I'd had any problems with Covid.

Only at the very start when a farmer's wife got upset. Since then everyone has been very supportive. I can't be any threat.

He works in a care home. We've had three deaths and staff off sick. We've both been tested and we're okay. Nevertheless after they'd gone I got out soap and washed my hands and the map.

I waited until families had left before erecting my tent on the grassy headland at the top of the falls. I've had time to kill between arriving at 4 and 7 when I cooked, so I sunbathed and ruminated, then fired up Dead Point by Peter Temple, an audio book on my iPhone. It's a perfectly beautiful evening,

*Benches and a place to camp at East Gill above Keld*

strong sun and a light breeze and the sound of the water and birdsong.

At midnight I was startled by a loud voice saying wake up, you're not allowed here. I shook myself out of slumber and poked my head out of the tent. A bright fluorescent light shone in my eyes.

I'm doing the Pennine Way. I'm 74.

You're not supposed to. I've rung the police.

I turned over and went back to sleep, reasonoing that the polic had better things to do than come and roust out a lone camper in the middle of the night. I heard no more of it and slept soundly.

*Camp on grassy headland above East Gill Falls*

# Day 12: Keld to Hearne Beck, Hardraw

**Sunday 31 May 2020   16.6 km, 10.3 miles**

Up by 5 and away before 6 and the sun hit me as I climbed the path from Keld, the day all shimmering and new. I was way above the gorge and Kidson Force and in the shadow of the limestone cliffs. On the hillside to the west the dotted farms and barns were caught in the bright morning light. A huge spider's web sparking with dew. A cuckoo sounded in the woods, birdsong – a chiffchaff. Rabbits scampering. A rabbit washing itself just in front of me and crows on patrol. Dead rabbits all along the path, shooting in the distance.

I reach Thwaite without incident along a fell track like those in the Lakes, although here the geology is limestone. I startled five brown heifers, one of which shot down the narrow walled lane and found herself trapped at a gate. I climbed the bank and gave it way and it scampered past in a flurry of hooves on the rocky surface.

*Sheep in the early dawn light above Kidson Side*

I stopped for breakfast on a grassy bank and made tea. Then again on a bench at the bus stop in Thwaite, admiring the renovated cottages all of which look like holiday homes. Directly in front of me there is a sign for Thwaitedale holiday cottages. The Kearton Country Hotel and Kearton Tearooms are closed and the traditional public telephone box disappointingly has a phone but no line. Time to set off up Shunner Fell.

I took a shortcut, marked to Shunner, across a flower meadow because it looked nice and soon gained the stony fell road and slogged up it. I met a couple coming down. They'd been wild camping on Shunner. They looked fairly experienced.

We started in Horton in Ribblesdale and will get a train back from Kirby Stephen. Are you going all the way? I told them about walking home. We live fairly close to the Way in Clitheroe.

There is no water up there, we found a spring.

There's good water in the beck before the village.

With this weather the only problem is the water.

Yes, water and a signal to ring my wife to tell her I'm all right. Do you use tablets?

No you have to take some risk. We thought we'd get away for a couple of

*Kearton Hotel and Tearooms, Thwaite, all closed*

days. Well you have to, don't you?

The path is flagged for much of the way across the fell and the final section to the top is cobbled. There is a cross shelter on the summit and I chose the quadrant most sheltered as there is a stiff chill breeze blowing. I thought to stop here for lunch but decided to continue down to get out of the wind. On the way down I met a young Brazilian. He had a large pack and was only doing part of the way. I don't have time he said.

I had to find water. From the map I'd seen a likely place on Hearn Beck and noted the wall leading down to the Old Coal Road and beyond to the stream. It was a steep descent and, on reaching the stream, which I feared looked dry from above, found it was flowing strongly. I followed its course to find a place to camp. The only catch was no signal. I decided to spend the afternoon here.

I had lunch, took off my clothes and had a sunbathe and another sleep. I woke and went to explore, leaving all my kit. I went down river round a few bends as far as some trees and shade, hoping to get a line of sight but got no welcoming beep from my phone. So I returned and climbed back the way I'd come and got a signal. I went back to the camp and washed including my hair, for the first time, filled my bottles, struggled back up the side of the ravine with my pack and found a place to camp on the top.

*Great Shunner Fell summit*

# Day 13: Hearne Beck to Cross Pot, Horton

**Monday 1 June 2020   25.4 km, 15.8 miles**

I woke at 6 after a disturbed night sliding down on the slope that hadn't looked much when I pitched the tent but, on the slippery ground sheet, was. So I didn't get away till after 8. It's an easy walk down to Hardraw, a pretty village, then along the water meadows to Hawes.

I noted the butchers, bakers, the pharmacy and grocery store before asking directions to the post office in the community centre set back off the main road in an alley. Hawes is a nice fell town, small but, with lots of rich second homeowners, very well appointed. I got the second box Ghazala had sent and transferred everything over and resent the box home with dirty clothes and food and stuff I didn't want. I asked the friendly woman at the entrance if I could leave my sack while I went shopping. First to the grocery store, which was like a deli and had cold meat and cheese counter, fresh fruit and veg and about 20 kinds of malt whiskey, many of which were new to me. I've bought

*Turfy Hill, Hawes, almost deserted when I first arrived*

Quicks extra mature cheddar, Parmesan and a pasty at the cheese counter, two Pink Lady apples and two nice looking oranges and a carrot and, to top it off, a chocolate tiffin for tea.

I went back and got my sack and ate an apple and an orange on the bench, savouring the juice, undecided whether I liked the orange this tart or would have preferred it sweeter. The centre manager was on his knees in his suit trousers measuring. Then he began to stick yellow circles 2 m apart in a line of dots.

Expecting more people I said.

It's the guidelines, he said, and asked me about my trip. You got the weather for it.

Hawes seems a nice town and amazingly well served.

Yes it is. But then anywhere would look good this weather.

It wasn't obvious finding the right alley by which to leave since it wasn't signposted and I went wrong in the meadows, seduced by a green path and a gate in the distance. An elderly couple had come over a stile and were watching me. She had a white printed dress and they both had big straw hats. They looked romantic floating above the field of buttercups. I thought of shouting, this is the path, thinking they'd stopped because they were lost.

*Community centre and Post office, Hawes, where I collected the second box ghazal sent*

*Looking back at St Margaret's Church, Hawes*

*I was a sucker for a broad green path that led me astray*

Good job I didn't because I found, a field or two later, that they'd been on the right path and me on the wrong one.

It's a steep slog up to Ten End with the heavy pack, seemingly so much heavier with all the new food and tucker. A young woman in skimpy shorts and top was collecting wool the sheep had cast. Her husband roared past on his quad bike. There were lots of building materials in their yard. A sign said they did self-catering at Gaudy Lane Farm. It looks as if he's extending his holdings. The lane changes to a steep grassy path. At the top of Ten End before the High Road I stopped for lunch – pasty, delicious, with apple and cheddar cheese.

Off again, startling the flock of 200-300 black headed gulls. The Cam High Road has a grassy verge at first but then narrows to a stony track with a stonewall to the right. I can see Ingleborough in the distance. It looks a long way but it will get nearer. I stumble on the stones. I stumble a lot, especially on the tussocky grass at campsites early in the morning. It would be so easy to fall and hurt myself. I fell in the river yesterday.

A huge brown hawk, flying low, at the T-junction on the High Road. In this section the road is quite transformed with a tarmac surface to take the heavy logging lorries. I can see a machine working on the edge of the forest below me. This is one of the places which has been totally transformed since we

*Cam High Road, Ingleborough in the far distance*

came on our circular walk round the Dales in 1986.

From Cam End it still seems never-ending. I filled my water bottles at Ling Gill. This is the only water before Malham Tarn. But I lost signal and had to keep going. I reasoned that there would be a signal at Withens where a short cut leaves the main way to Horton. I said to myself, over that shoulder you will get a signal and I did.

I rang Scharlie and had a chat, then set about finding a site, eventually settling on the edge of a limestone pavement as the only flat bit I could find. I remember the clints and grykes from geography at school; grykes being the fissures between the clints or lumps of limestone. I unpacked and found I had lost my pheasant feather. I was upset and went to look where I'd taken off my pack but to no avail. Bad luck? I'm not superstitious but I regret its loss.

*Ling Gill, where I stopped for a rest and where I think I lost the pheasant tail feather*

# Pennine Way South

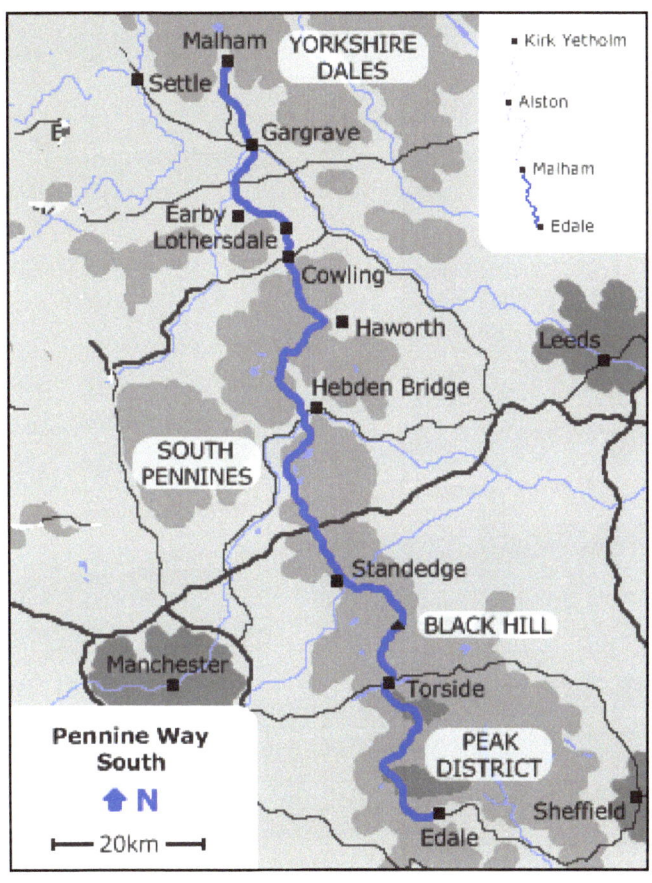

# Day 14: Cross Pot to Gargrave

**Tuesday 2 June 2020  34.7 km, 21.5 miles**

I had a good night and woke at 5 was away by 6. The path up PenyGhent (the Hill of Winds) has been machined to death since we were here, with gravel and huge stone steps leading to the summit. There is a new stone shelter and seat at the trig point and I stopped awhile and had breakfast. A succession of walkers had passed me on the ascent and more went past now, more than I've seen on the whole of the rest of the trip so far. PenyGhent is popular! I chatted to the last two. They came from Bowland and are doing the Three Peaks. They said they wanted to do the Pennine Way. We talked about walking in Bowland and how it was underrated and how it was only opened up in the last 10 years.

I set off. When Scharlie and I did it years ago, coming off PenyGhent, instead of following the main path south, we headed straight across Fawcetts Moor making a beeline for the track up Fountains fell. I don't know how we did it.

*Camp on the limestone pavement at Cross Pot*

Looking back it looked too steep to descend the cliffs and there was no sign of a path across the boggy moor. Today, I followed the main way and it was tricky coming down and you had to be careful not to slip. Looking back you can see the geology – a band of sandstone capping the band of limestone. And you appreciate this on the way down. First, crumbly sandstone with lots of loose grit to cause a slip. Then limestone, worn smooth by many feet, treacherous in the wet. I met more people coming up. This is the way most people do PenyGhent, not the way I'm going. An old boy stopped to let me get past, saying it was an excuse for a rest. He looked anxious watching me tripping down.

The rough track that follows is a byway and is blocked by big stones and a chain. Two shepherds or gamekeepers in a mini-mog neatly avoided the rocks and zoomed past. On the road you pass a well appointed farm called Rainscar sheltered by a stand of sycamore.

The path up the fell is fairly steep but easy and I found a tiny beck and refilled my bottles. It is extremely hot and hard going, and I need the water. I'm drinking 3 L a day. The path goes close to numerous mineshafts. Maybe they were mining lead like in Derbyshire. But this was small-scale workings, whereas in Winster, where we lived once, the mines were big operations.

*PenyGhent from the south showing the gritstone and limestone layers*

Eventually I reach Malham Tarn. You see a place in the distance, a settlement you're trying to reach and in this case the tarn, and it seems to take for ages to get there. I'm moving fairly freely now and am not so preoccupied with how my body is doing. Nevertheless, I stop to check when I feel a boot rubbing and take it off and rearrange my socks rather than wait till it's too late and I've got a blister.

This is rich farming country with lush pastures and fat looking sheep and cattle. There are people out and about and I do my best to keep my distance. Then the path narrows down the defile of Ing Scar. I remembered the long, flat grassy stretches between here and the tarn from 1986. No one about then. Flat grassy paths between Malham Tarn and Malham Cove

You cross the limestone pavement at the top of the cliff of Malham Cove and descend steeply on stone steps. I stopped, walking back into the cliff face to reach the spring source and clean water – there were dozens of families lower down playing in the stream. I made tea and ate a late lunch. Two Pakistani gentlemen admired my stove and tea making and said they would come better prepared next time. Then the troop of Pakistani young women and children asked me directions and we chatted. They were from Barnsley and had just moved to Bradford. I'm not sure about Yorkshire yet and I'm

*Malham Cove where I stop for a late lunch and make tea*

missing Lancashire, said one.

There was no shop in Malham village and there was a queue for the ice cream stall and although I wanted one I didn't want to wait in line. A couple sitting outside the pub, him showing off his red Triumph motorcycle, asked me about the solar panel on my pack. I've had it on since bad weather is coming and I needed a full charge. Unfortunately things didn't go to plan.

From Malham you walk along water meadows of the River Aire, passing through the expensive looking village of Hanlith and then a huge mill like building at eight Airton bridge. I wonder what it was once? (I learn later that this was a cotton mill, built on land originally oened by Bolton Priory and that it produced Dettol during WW2. I also learn Airton had a large Quaker community in the 1800s.) Soon after I run into two young men doing the Way, the first I'd seen. They said they were doing it in 2-3 days stages, using two cars.

Were you in Greg's Hut? When we were there we were blown off our feet and bent double.

I know, I said, I read what you wrote in the hut log.

They asked how I was getting on and were intrigued by how I've managed to do it all in one hit. They were Poles and asked if I'd been to the Tatras

Yes, in 2009, but from the Slovak side. I climbed Krivan.

*Zbyszek and Piotr, Poles doing the Way in stages*

They're been walking in the Lakes – Great Langdale, Red Pike and Honister Pass and want to go to the Peak District. They asked about routes. We took photographs of each other. I should have taken their email. I passed a man and a young child also doing the way in one-day stages, his wife picking them up at the end of each day.

I had to get my skates on. The Poles had told me that there was a Co-op in Gargrave that stayed open until 8. I was short of water for tomorrow and could buy some there. So I speeded up, making good time across Eastern Moor, avoiding getting lost and doing the next 3 miles in just over an hour.

Gargrave is quite large and well appointed. I make camp in the wooden shelter at the crossroads in the centre near the bridge. I checked the phone box and it worked and the loos were open and very clean, so I washed. Then I went shopping. I bought smoked mackerel, Greek yoghurt and raspberries for tonight's dinner. Two apples and two oranges, a carton of orange juice and two large bottles of water. I needed a plastic bag to carry them all in. Then I went back to the shelter and repacked, decanting the water into my own bottles. I rang Scharlie reverse charges. She answered but put the phone down, thinking it was a scam call. So I texted her to tell her what I was doing and she answered. I was contemplating stopping in the shelter and sleeping on

*Leeds-Liverpool Canal, Gargrave*

a bench because heavy rain was forecast, but it was too public and the bench was too narrow. So I walked to the church to see if it had a large porch. No luck. I was tempted by the grassy bank and lawn next to the river but again it was too public, fronted by a line of houses. So I followed the Way and right at the start in the first field I came to, I found a spot in the corner, overlooked by a house, but hopefully okay. I've had my delicious meal and I'm ready for bed. It's just started to rain heavily, 10 o'clock.

*Camp in the corner of this field in Gargrave, where I had my best night's sleep*

# Day 15: Gargrave to Heptonstall Moor

**Wednesday 3 June 2020  39.2 km, 24.4 miles**

I woke at 4 but went back to sleep till 5, by which time it was raining. I'd had a good night, undisturbed but for the chiming of the church clock. The tent was soaked and I packed it in the rain and set off across the fields. It's complex and somewhat unsatisfying traversing rich agricultural land – pastures with sheep and cattle. You go through East Marton and Thornton in Craven, both villages that look pleased with themselves.

I rescued another lamb that had stuck its head through a wire mesh fence to reach the more succulent grass on the other side and had got its horns jammed – easy to go in but difficult to get out. You have to hold on tight then work the horns out of the trap. There followed a patch of moor at Elslack with a mini top at Pinshaw. You follow the Skipton and Liverpool Canal a short way. A sign said, Liverpool 89 miles. There was no one about and no barges moving. You would have thought this would be a good time to journey but maybe it's the no overnight stay rule or maybe all the pubs shut. I always suspected that

*Cowling*

stopping at country pubs was the main reason people went on canal holidays.

It was a long day. I was determined to reach Heptonstall, near Hebden Bridge. You go through Cowling – more downmarket and industrial, and no second homes. It's a long strung out village with a large chimney. There are lots of wind turbines – small ones in farmers' fields.

It was lunchtime and there was a shelter on the A6068, so I stopped and made coffee. I had paused earlier at Surgill Beck and had an orange and half an oat bar, but there was nowhere to rest in the rain. Now I had apple and cheese for lunch. Ickornshaw Moor is quite remote and the path narrow. You drop down to Ponden Reservoir and then climb steeply via Buckley to famous Withins Height. Famous because it is thought to be the setting of Wuthering Heights. Howarth, were the Brontës lived, is just nearby.

They go in for giant steps here – most tiring. I also have to take great care on the stiles because it's easy to slip. There is a line of a dozen hutments on the way up Withins, all of a pattern, although the details and materials differ. A simple shed with a pitched roof, windows barred with drop-down shutters from inside, a wheelbarrow outside, for collecting peat I imagine, since all have stove pipes or chimney stacks. All have water butts to collect rain for drinking. No one about and little sign any one has been here for a while. Then

*One of the dozen hutments on the way up Withens fell*

a renovated luxury place housing architects and a bespoke joiners.

The path winds up, flagged with stone, to Top Withens, the inspiration for the isolated farmhouse of Wuthering Heights. I must read it; it's on my iPhone. On the fell above a young man on a quad bike thundered down towards me. We chatted. He is an apprentice gamekeeper and lives near the reservoir. He had a rifle in the cradle across the tank of the quad bike and various baskets and containers that may have held traps and bait. I imagine he'd been checking the traps. I asked him what he was after. Crows and such, he said.

I passed two more reservoirs with little water. A goose landed like a seaplane, flaring to land. I got a bit anxious from here to Gorple Lower, feeling I'd gone wrong since the sign said byway. But it was fine, and I stopped because I had a signal and thought to camp. But once I opened my phone I'd lost it. So I opted to continue and try to cross Heptonstall fell before it got too late. At one point I realised I was singing It's a long way to Tipperary in my head. The sun came out briefly so I got out the panel, but with little effect.

The moor was surprisingly easy and I made camp at the end of it, putting up the wet tent and making supper sitting on a handy bench above Heptonstall. I texted Scharlie to tell her all was well.

*Top Withins, rumoured to be the inspiration for Wuthering Heights*

*Plaque about Emily Bronte's, Wuthering Heights*

*Camp above Heponstall*

# Day 16: Heptonstall to Wessenden Reservoir

**Thursday 4 June 2020   35.9 km, 22.3 miles**

I had a more difficult night, feeling cold till I put on my duvet jacket. It's hard when everything is damp or wet. I rigged up a line for my socks, more on principle than in any hope they might dry. Still it kept them off the damp tent floor. I woke at 4 and again at 5 and got up in the usual way. My feet are sore from yesterday and I had two blisters so my first task was to use the second skin Ghazala had given me to fashion plasters. I also put on fresh socks as the others are worn and damp.

I made breakfast, but frustratingly can't find my spoon, so I ate my muesli with my pocketknife – carefully. I sat contemplating the route. It's all high moor from now on, so another cold night to come. Wish the sun would come out so I can charge my phone. The phone is both a blessing and a curse. One more thing to worry about. In the past I was away for three or four weeks and maybe sent a postcard.

*Hebble Hole, Golden Water, near Jack bridge*

I left in good order but crossing the Calder Valley is complex and involves a lot of up and down. I couldn't initially see where to go when I left the moor and reached the road. I figured I needed to go west away from Hebden Bridge, but was undecided, looking at the map, when a bus stopped and the driver offered to help.

Pennine Way, I said.

200 yards up the road. Hop on and I'll take you.

You're aiming for the monument, Stoodley Pike, once you're there it's flat.

You drop down to a lovely dell near Jack Bridge, where I had intended to spend the night, then up the steepest, narrowest cobbled lane imaginable between stonewalls that climbs high to the first ridge. It's rather charming but wet from ferns and foliage. Then you drop down again steeply through woods.

The inhabitants seem to follow the alternative lifestyle Hebden Bridge is famous for and Scharlie would be pleased at the wild gardening everyone does round here. There is also evidence of people being at home and living outdoors over the past few weeks, with tables chairs and barbecues scattered about.

This is a busy valley, carrying the A646, the Calder Valley rail line, the river and the Rochdale Canal. After crossing all of them the track winds up through

*Narrow walled lane up Pry Hill*

Callis Wood to where the Hebden Bridge loop diverges. I should have continued on the track but was seduced by a sign saying Stoodley Pike and a broad grassy track. I'm a sucker for grassy tracks. I realised I had gone wrong after a while but rather than go back I opted to go over Edge Moor and to get onto the moor I had to climb a fence. There was no path but I could see where I was aiming for and rejoined the Way at the end of the dirt road. So although I climbed higher, the going had been easier.

Finally I reached Stoodley Pike. I could see the black obelisk easily from where I was camped but it had taken me 3 1/2 hours and I thought at times that I'd never get here. Apart from this useless monolith to human folly, not even a bench to sit and admire the view.

Leaving Stoodley Pike is as hard as getting there, since you seem to see it for ages. I nearly went wrong again, when instead of following the edge I deviated to the left on a grassy path expecting it to come round but it didn't, leaving me disorientated until I worked my way back to the main path. At the reservoir I finally lost sight of the blessed monument and had a long stretch of flat embankment, easy but tiring on the feet. I stopped to chat to a man who looked like a walker about my age. He said he'd done the Pennine Way three times, although always south to north.

*Stoodley Pike (1,300 ft) a black obelisk commemorating defeat of Napoleon 1814*

I'm 72 and my family say I'm too old to do it again.

I'm 74.

Oh my! Well done.

I asked about streams and he said they were all dry and only puddles. Have you a filter? You can get water at the reservoir.

No.

He offered me his second bottle but found he'd left it in the car. He gave me directions past the White House, a famous public house, currently closed and onto Blackstone Edge. The trig point is on the lower of the two summit blocks. The higher is called Robin Hood's bed. It has a 7' × 2' depression on the top. Then the Roman Road, although that is disputed. If you want to do it again in a couple weeks I'm your man. If we keep social distance can I shake your hand, he said, putting out his paw.

How does that work? I thought. Nevertheless I shook. He seemed very chuffed.

Camping he asked.

Yes.

Oh my!

A skein of half a dozen barnacle geese flew over and landed in formation

Blackstone Edge summit

on the reservoir. I tried filling my bottles, but the water was cloudy with peat. I thought I'd ask for water at the White House. Two men were repairing the flat roof and let me fill my bottles at the outside tap.

Climbing up to Blackstone edge my rucksack felt heavy with the extra 3L. I still didn't know where I was going to spend the night. The next few miles and all the rest of the Way is exposed and the weather forecast poor. Blackstone Edge was windy but I found a cleft where I could hide from the wind and have a late lunch of ham.

From Blackstone Edge the path is flagged up White Hill and the going is easy and you plod on. I'm broken in now and my mind doesn't harp on about pains or counting to 50. It just wanders. From there you cross a moor to the sound of traffic on the M62 and then the motorway on a footbridge – quite surreal after the solitude, to see the busy rush of life.

There is easy walking across Buckstones Moss. I felt tired and wondered where I'd get to tonight. So I stopped and made a brew and had an oat bar and decided to try and get to the good campsite north of Crowdon. This is country I know. Standedge is gritstone, as are our edges.

Wessenden Moor is huge and coming down steps towards the reservoir I met two men. They asked if I was doing the Pennine. They waited at the

*Plenty of wind turbines break the sky-line*

bottom for me. I was tired and my legs felt like giving way on the big steps. They asked if I wanted a shortcut and suggested that instead of going down to the valley floor and climbing back up to the track I could contour round into the next clough and reach the head of the dam and cross it and regain the path. It seemed a long way but it was level and very pretty.

It was now just after 7 and I began to realise that I would either need to find somewhere to camp or do Black Hill in the dark. Everywhere was steep and exposed and no signal. So I climbed up the path towards the A635 where I could see vehicles passing on the skyline.

The phone pinged and I knew I had a signal. Soon after there was a bench with a view of the dams and a flat bit of grass so I decided to stop and make camp. I ate ham and cheese while I waited for the kettle boil to make my sweet and sour chicken with rice and sweet tea. Scharlie texted to say rain and 50 mile an hour winds from the West Northwest were forecast for tomorrow. So much for plans of meeting me with a flask and having a picnic at the Mill Pond.

*Crossing the M62*

# Day 16: Wessenden to Edale

**Friday 5 June 2020  38.8 km, 24.1 miles**

Woke to heavy rain and low mist. I studied the map and wrote out compass bearings. I had somehow lost my compass yesterday. I was upset about it and had gone back a way to find it. I figured I must have lost it when I stopped for tea on White Hill when I was feeling downcast. It wasn't that I didn't think I could manage without it. I had a compass on my phone, although it wasn't as useful as the Silva system it would do. It was what the loss signified. Each time I stopped anywhere I was so careful to check the ground before setting off. A moment's inattention, a lack of care, and something went wrong. Not catastrophic in this case, but it could be. I'm travelling with the minimum of gear and each item of kit seems essential. Never mind. Stop beating yourself up and get on.

The rain stopped as I packed and the sky had cleared by the time I left at 6.20. At the road I was confused by a stile with a yellow marker but soon

*Dean Clough, luckily not in spate*

figured I had to walk further up the road to the A635.

The path up the Black Hill starts easy but then becomes unrelenting. My usual curlew followed me. There were compost bin butts to my right and a warning about crossing the river in spate, although it is no torrent despite the heavy rain. Following the long drought, the water is brown with peat. I stop at a sinkhole and see the peat is 7 foot deep at least.

I reached the flat summit with its bright white trig point and survey what's ahead of me on Bleaklow and Kinder. Looking back, I could see a couple of ranges the way I'd come. It would be nice to see it all laid out in a bird's view panorama. As I walk I try and remember what happened after such a place and where I stayed the night before last. It is difficult to make your brain work while you're walking. For example doing mental arithmetic. I worked out that I'd done the first half to Middleton in 9 1/2 days so about 14 miles a day, and the second half in seven days, about 20 miles a day. I had savoured the first half more. It was more challenging and interesting. I have also been doing much longer days this second half.

Black Hill over, you descend Crowden Clough, walk along the top of Laddow Rocks, being careful not to trip, and follow the valley down to the Woodhead Pass Road. I could see the line of the first part of the ascent on the other

*Black Hill summit*

side of the valley. The weather was at once sun, then showers, with the wind gradually picking up.

The way crosses the valley on the dam, but there was a large locked gate and a notice saying the Pennine Way was closed due to maintenance work and those wishing to cross should use a detour down the valley. I could see orange clad man pouring concrete. I thought I haven't come all this way to be stopped now. So I climbed the barrier then a fence and walked down to the dam. The man on the mixer called the foreman over and I explained I'd come all the way from Scotland and was nearly home and could he please let me cross. He looked back at the men wading in 6 to 9 inches of wet concrete and said, not this way. If you climb over the railings you can walk along the grass face of the dam. And that's what I did.

The climb up Torside Clough was one of the longest of the trip and towards the top it wasn't obvious which way to go. I opted for the higher path. At the top, looking back, I could see it would be easier coming down because you would see either path would do. But there was also an option to take a broader path, which diverged to go to shooting buttes and would have got me lost.

*Torside Reservoir, Woodhead Pass*

*Paths at top of Torside Clough*

*Bleaklow Head (633 m)*

The weather had turned savage – very cold, strong wind and hail, which stung my cheeks and bare legs. I got to the summit of Bleaklow Head, what an appropriate name, and was feeling pleased I'd made it in such poor conditions, when a girl in a pink jacket with three-quarter length tights popped up and asked me if I knew were the crash site was. She looked like she'd gone for a walk in the park.

Eventually I made it to the A57 Snake Road and crossed and continued on the other side. I rested in a dip in the heather to eat my last oat bar before tackling the pull from the col after Mill Hill. The wind was really savage now coming from the west and threatening to blow me off my feet. In fact, it knocked me over once or twice. Finally I reached Kinder Downfall. A lamb was bleating most pitifully, having lost its mother. I know how you feel I thought.

I have walked this way numerous times and I remembered it as quite short. Today it seemed endless. Between the trig point and Jacob's Ladder the wind redoubled its efforts to destroy me. A fitting Pennine Way finale I thought. The sun shone briefly on the valley sides as I descended Jacob's Ladder but disappeared each time I got my camera out. I had a strange sensation that somebody was following me closely, just over my left shoulder and turned to

*Kinder Downfall*

see but there was no one. I've have this feeling a number of times on the walk.

On the way down a couple asked me what I thought was the best bit. I struggled to answer – so many things, no one thing. It's as if on a long trip like this many things happen, too many detailed experiences for the mind to hold. They merge and blend. This was an exceptional time. No one else was doing the Way, and very few people were about, either on the hill or in the villages. It was like a sci-fi movie. At times the solitude, the wildness and the contact with the elements was so intense as to leave me breathless. For most people, doing the way would have been a convivial experience – companionship, meeting other walkers, cafes, and pubs. My experience was totally different. Deeply satisfying and at times, in the evening looking for somewhere to camp or getting lost, anxious making.

I'd done it. Slowly, but done it well, in good style and in a decent time. And I've experienced a lot, know more about nature, geology, local history of the places and counties I'd walked through, and it had reaffirmed my understanding that putting one foot in front of the other and keeping going you accomplish great things.

The Pennine Way is wild in the sense that it is unpopulated and in time of Covid, devoid of people. And because of this you see a lot of nature and its

*Packhorse bridge at bottom of Jacob's Ladder*

workings. But it is not a wilderness. The whole way you see the hand of man shaping the environment. Even on the open moors' great tracts you see that men have created this habitat to run sheep and shoot grouse. They burnt and chopped, built paths and bridges. And in the pastures, walls hedges and fences divide the fields. The settlements, their location, form and material are defined by the topography and geology on which they sit and contrived by the wit and will of people over a long history. You feel this in the rusty latch of a gate, the stonewall of a barn, the quarries and the mineshafts, the drovers' roads and the pathways marking the desire lines of rural life. I became a connoisseur of stiles and bridges; some well contrived, others less so. My legs are not as strong as they were, the steps on the stiles too high both up and down, the stone slippy with centuries of wear. So I had to take uncommon care not to slip. Nevertheless I made it without mishap.

At Barbour Booth I rang Scharlie to meet me in Edale car park while I walked the last mile and a half. Never has a mile seemed so long.

*Edale*

# Route map

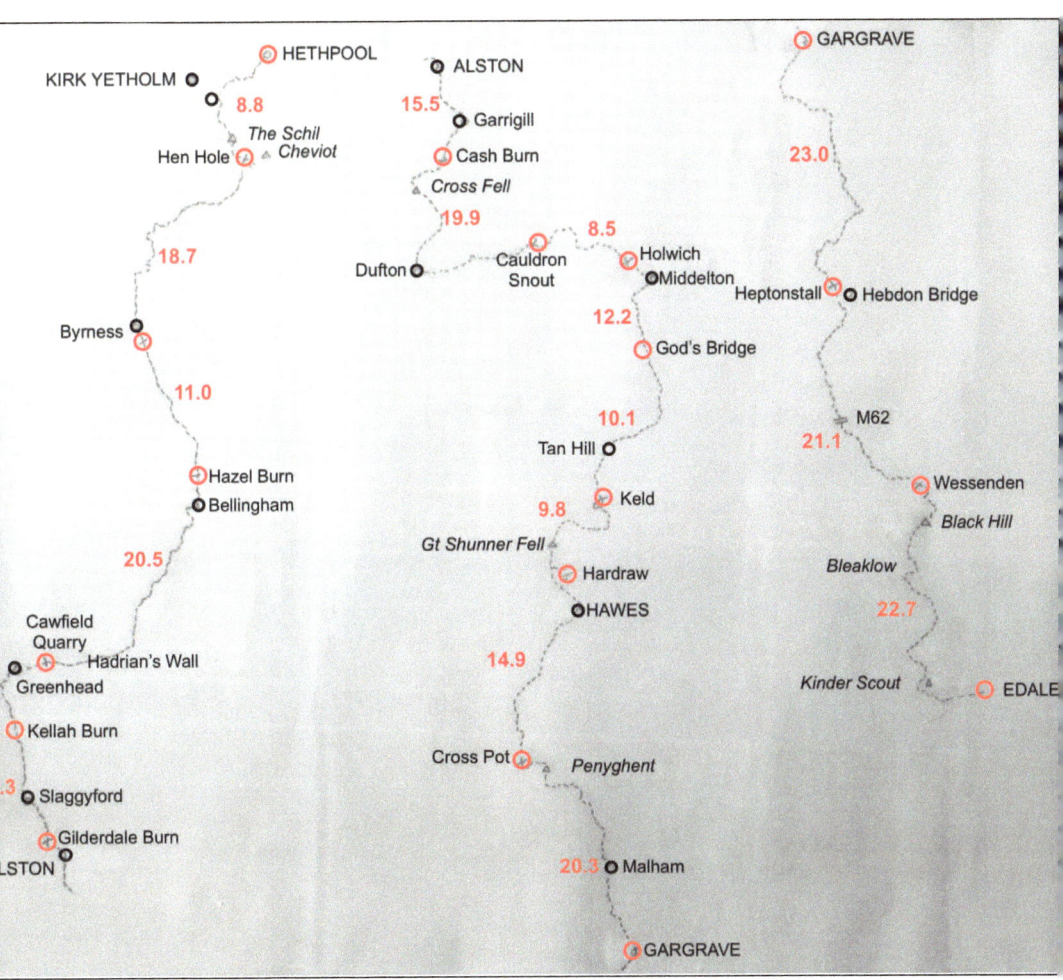

*Map of route showing distance walked each day in miles*

# Itinerary

| Day | | Date | Start | Finish | Km | Miles |
|---|---|---|---|---|---|---|
| 1 | Wed | 20-May | Hethpool | Hen Hole | 14.2 | 8.8 |
| 2 | Thu | 21-May | Hen Hole | Byrness | 30.1 | 18.7 |
| 3 | Fri | 22-May | Byrness | Hazel Burn, Bellingham | 17.7 | 11.0 |
| 4 | Sat | 23-May | Hazel Burn | Cawfield Quarry, Hadrians Wall | 33.0 | 20.5 |
| 5 | Sun | 24-May | Cawfield Quarry | Kellah Burn, Upham | 13.9 | 8.6 |
| 6 | Mon | 25-May | Kellah Burn | Gilderdale Burn, Alston | 8.6 | 5.3 |
| 7 | Tue | 26-May | Gilderdale Burn | Cash Burn, Garrigill | 24.9 | 15.5 |
| 8 | Wed | 27-May | Cash Burn | Cauldron Snout | 32.0 | 19.9 |
| 9 | Thu | 28-May | Cauldron Snout | Holwich, Teesdale | 13.7 | 8.5 |
| 10 | Fri | 29-May | Holwich | Gods Bridge | 19.6 | 12.2 |
| 11 | Sat | 30-May | God's Bridge | Keld | 16.2 | 10.1 |
| 12 | Sun | 31-May | Keld | Hearne Beck, Hardraw | 15.7 | 9.8 |
| 13 | Mon | 01-Jun | Hearne Beck | Cross Pot, Horton | 24.0 | 14.9 |
| 14 | Tue | 02-Jun | Cross Pot | Gargrave | 32.7 | 20.3 |
| 15 | Wed | 03-Jun | Gargrave | Heptonstall Moor | 37.0 | 23.0 |
| 16 | Thu | 04-Jun | Heptonstall | Wessenden Reservoir | 33.9 | 21.1 |
| 17 | Fri | 05-Jun | Wessenden | Edale | 36.6 | 22.7 |
| TOTAL | | | | | 403.8 | 250.9 |

There is a slight discrepancy between my measurement of the distance covered (251 miles) and the usually accepted distance (270 miles). I used a map wheel with 1:40,000 maps to measure the distance each day and compared this to Strava measurements for some of the stages. I calculate a total of 251 miles (404 km).

The distance chart in the Mountain Refuge Hut near Hen Hole puts the total at 267 miles (429 km) and the Pennine Way Guide by Stuart Greig and Henry Stedman has 253 miles

# Kit List

| Item | Make Model | Notes | Weight | Stars |
|---|---|---|---|---|
| Rucksack | Lightwave U1 | Excellent, durable, light. Could do with larger side pockets | 993 | *** |
| Tent | Nordisk Telemark 2 | Fantastic light tent, very waterproof, Attached extra guys | 950 | *** |
| Sleeping bag | Vango Ultralight Pro 100 | Light but poor; couldn't cope with cold nights | 937 | *** |
| Mat | Thermarest Prolite 3 ladies | Good, old so may be better options | 620 | ** |
| Stove / pan | Jetboil Primus | Excellent system; fast, light and packs small | 326 | *** |
| Gaz | Nalgene 48 oz | Good | 180 | *** |
| Water canteen | Platyus | Excellent flexible fold up version, filled when lack of streams | 24 | *** |
| Water bottle | Strathmore | Good, works well | 100 | *** |
| Water bottle | Gerber | Disposable bottle, goes on all my walks | 15 | |
| Knife | Paraframe mini | Excellent, light and very sharpenable | 55 | *** |
| Lighter | Torjet | Excellent, better than Bic | 21 | *** |
| First aid kit | Boots | Good, added compeed, second skin, arnica, | 123 | *** |
| Note book | Moleskin | I always use this make for my journals | 111 | *** |
| Pens | Biro | Excellent | 22 | *** |
| Phone | iPhone SE | Would have preferred a longer battery life | 75 | ** |
| Battery/cable | Jackery 22 wh | Poor, only gave 1-2 charges | 173 | * |
| Solar panel | Anker PowerPort | Excellent. Fast when sun out. Could be strapped to rucksac | 226 | *** |
| Sun glasses | | Excellent cheap TK Max glasses | 25 | |
| Camera | Olympus VR-370 | Worked well; reasonably good quality photos | 173 | ** |
| Spare batteries | Duracell DR9686 | Each lasted more than 6 days | 15 | ** |
| Maps | Harvey Pennine Way N/S | Excellent, very accurate, durable and easy to use | 46 | *** |
| Compass | Silva | Excellen, very practical, have always used Silva | 42 | ** |
| Headtorch | Petzl e+lite | Excellent, very light and powerful LED | 26 | *** |
| Spare batteries | Duracell | Unnecessary | 8 | |
| Debit card | | Essential | 1 | |
| Eye mask | | Found I didn't need, sleeping and waking with sun | 8 | |
| Dry bags | Sea to Summit | Excellent, durable and completely waterproof | 310 | *** |
| Anorak | Arcteryx | Orange | 506 | *** |
| Fleece | Berghaus Alpha SV | Windproof with hood | 518 | *** |
| Duvet | Marmot Chaleco | Excellent, down very warm | 412 | *** |
| Cap | North face | Excellent, old friend | 86 | *** |
| Boots | Meindl Bhutan | Excellent, especially for my wider bunyioned feet | 1964 | *** |
| Gaiters | Sea to Summit | Good, light but still got damp socks. | 110 | ** |
| Walking poles | Black Diamond Distance flz | Excellent, light and well balanced | 384 | *** |
| Sandals | Clogs | Useful in camp for tired feet | 296 | *** |
| Overtousers | Beghaus Gortex Paclite | Didn't use and sent back in post restante box | 204 | ** |
| Pants | Kühl | Excellent, fit well and good pockets | 351 | *** |
| Shorts | Haglofs | Excellent, love the extra front pockets | 299 | *** |
| T shirts | Adidas | Excellent, stayed looking smart | 150 | *** |
| Gloves | Lowe Alpine | Didn't use and sent back in box, regretted on last day | 22 | ** |
| Inner socks | Coolmax | These are very old and I should have bought new | 104 | ** |
| Outer socks | Bridgedale | Excellent, very comfortable | | *** |
| Underpants | M&S | | 46 | |
| Belt | Nylon webbing | Essential, because you loose weight (6-7 kilos) | 25 | |
| Tent repair | | Unnecessary in the event | 14 | |
| Water purification | Oasis | Necessary if wild camping and getting water from streams | 2 | *** |
| Oats/dried fruit | | Jumbo oats with nuts and dried fruit - raisins, apple and banana | 560 | *** |
| Freeze dried packs | Expedition | Excellent, especially fish and potato, Thai chicken and veg | 200 | ** |
| Dried banana | | Excellent snack | 210 | ** |
| Oat bars | Trek | Excellent energy giving snack | 24 | *** |
| Cured ham | Basco Lomo embuchado | Excellent, sliced very thin. Kept well | 480 | ** |
| Tea bags | Yorkshire | Excellent | 34 | *** |
| Coffee | Nescafe Gold | Poor | 10 | * |
| Sugar, salt, pepper | | Didn't take enough sugar | 30 | |
| Lip salve | Soltan factor 30 | | 7 | |
| Sun cream | Nivea Sun 30 | | 45 | |
| Toothpaste | | | 15 | |
| Toothbrush | CuraProX | | 10 | |
| Soap | Go | Fag end on a used bar | 12 | |
| Towel | Micro fibre | Mini | 42 | |
| Toilet paper | | End of a roll | 30 | |
| Contact lens/drops | | | 21 | |
| Spectacles | | | 70 | |
| Foot rasp | | Sent back in box | 76 | |
| TOTAL | | | 13 kg | |

# Training walks

| Date | Title | Time | Distance ml | Elevation ft | Notes |
|---|---|---|---|---|---|
| Mon, 16/03/2020 | Stanage Edge-Rivelin Valley | 05:01 | 11.99 | 1,370 | Packed rucksack with what I intended to carry on walk. Bubbling call of curlew at Overstones Farm. Russet winged kestrel hovering over High Neb. Tired by Redmires and staggered along Stanage. |
| Fri, 20/03/2020 | Burbage-Higgar Tor | 02:58 | 6.55 | 1,006 | Lunch in a hollow below Carl Wark. Returned down Callow Bank via hutments below Overstones to our lane. |
| Sun, 22/03/2020 | Totley-Blacka Moor | 01:33 | 3.49 | 392 | A walk with Scharlie on chilly day. Soft spot in the heather on Totley Moor for a lunch on home made pizza. Pretty views from Blacka Hill to Burbage and Hallam Moors. Two girls racing their horses. |
| Mon, 23/03/2020 | Win Hill - Ladybower | 03:46 | 10.13 | 1,198 | Parked in Quaker Community and walked along old railway line. Picnic on top of Win Hill followed by a pleasant walk along the ridge, drop to Ladybower and a long walk back along the reservoir. |
| Wed, 25/03/2020 | Stanage-Bamford Edge | 04:22 | 9.43 | 1,381 | Familiar walk along Stanage but left edge early and had to pick my way across boggy ground to path along Bamford Edge and back via usual path through Green's, MillPond, Warren and Cattside Moor. |
| Sun, 05/04/2020 | Scaperlow-Highlow | 03:47 | 8.61 | 1,588 | Along our lane and pretty path to Toothill Farm and Mitchell Field. Then Scraperlow and new lane down to Hathersage Booths and on to Highlow Hall. Back via Airman's Barn and path above the Dale. |
| Tue, 07/04/2020 | Cowclose-Hurst Clough | 02:43 | 5.91 | 1,226 | Investigated barn conversion below Carr Head Rocks and continued via Cow Close Farm and croissed valley to Birley Farm and Thorpe Farm. Clambered up Hurst Clough and returned via the Warren. |
| Wed, 15/04/2020 | Eyam Moor | 02:37 | 6.62 | 990 | A relaxed circular walk around Eyam Moor, visiting stone circle and returning via trig point on Sir William Hill |
| Sun, 19/04/2020 | Jacob's Ladder - Brown Knoll | 02:20 | 6.38 | 1,133 | Parked in Barbour Booth. Easy walk up Jacob's Ladder and kept to path over Brown Knoll where I'd gone in up to my thighs one winter. |
| Mon, 20/04/2020 | Bradwell Moor-Moss Rake | 02:33 | 6.45 | 688 | Walk with Scharlie to investigate possible site for wind turbine on Bradwell Moor and rewilding of Moss Rake. |
| Tue, 21/04/2020 | Ashop Clough-The Edge-Fairbrook | 03:54 | 9.34 | 1,517 | Stopped in carpark a mile above Snake Pass Inn. Hen Harrier in Ashop Clough. Very strong east wind along The Edge to Fairbrook Naze. |
| Thu, 23/04/2020 | Redmires-Rud Hill | 03:23 | 9.01 | 980 | A new walk for me over moor north of Ringinglow and Burbage Moor. |
| Sat, 25/04/2020 | Sir William Hill | 04:50 | 1.94 | 295 | A short walk with Scharlie up Sir William Hill |
| Sat, 02/05/2020 | Axe Edge Moor | 02:27 | 6.44 | 805 | A drive over to Buxton and a new walk on Axe Edge Moor |
| Wed, 06/05/2020 | Grindsbrook-Jaggers Clough | 03:50 | 9.76 | 1,599 | Park at Edale car park and tough climb up Grindsbrook followed by walk along edge and back along valley. |

# Peak training walk photos

*Measuring distances with a digital map wheel after I got back*

www.ingramcontent.com/pod-product-compliance
Lightning Source LLC
Chambersburg PA
CBHW041622220426
43662CB00001B/25